Twayne's English Authors Series

Sylvia E. Bowman, *Editor*

INDIANA UNIVERSITY

Owen Felltham

TEAS 189

Engraved title page of the 8th edition of Felltham's *Resolves* (1661), executed by Robert Vaughan. This design was used for all seventeenth-century editions of *Resolves* except the first.

OWEN FELLTHAM

By TED-LARRY PEBWORTH
The University of Michigan — Dearborn

TWAYNE PUBLISHERS
A DIVISION OF G. K. HALL & CO., BOSTON

Library of Congress Cataloging in Publication Data

Pebworth, Ted-Larry.
  Owen Felltham.

  (Twayne's English authors series ; TEAS 189)
  Bibliography: p. 141 - 44.
  Includes index.
  1. Feltham, Owen, 1602?-1668.
PR2270.F37Z8   828'.4'09 [B]   76-4863
ISBN 0-8057-6655-3

PR
2270
.F37
Z8

In memory of my teacher and friend

E. L. MARILLA
1900 - 1970

*Quid enim aliud es, quam ex omnia bonarum
artium ingenio collecta perfectio?*

Contents

About the Author

Ted-Larry Pebworth is Associate Professor of English and former Chairman of Humanities at the University of Michigan - Dearborn. He earned his B. A. (Honors) at Centenary College, his M. A. at Tulane University, and his Ph. D. at Louisiana State University. His doctoral dissertation, directed by the late E. L. Marilla, was a critical edition of Owen Felltham's *Resolves*. Before coming to Michigan, he taught at Louisiana State and at the University of Illinois at Chicago Circle.

Dr. Pebworth's essays and reviews have appeared in leading scholarly journals, including *English Language Notes*, *The Explicator*, *Journal of English and Germanic Philology*, *The Library*, *Papers on Language and Literature*, *Publications of the Modern Language Association*, *Romance Notes*, and *Seventeenth-Century News*. He is also an Assistant Editor of *Seventeenth-Century News*. He is the author of "An Annotated Bibliography of Owen Felltham," *Bulletin of the New York Public Library* (1976); co-editor (with Claude J. Summers) of *The Poems of Owen Felltham* (University Park, Pa., 1973); and General Editor of "An Annotated Bibliography of Robert Herrick," in *Trust to Good Verses: Herrick Tercentenary Essays* (Pittsburgh, 1976). He is currently working on a book-length critical history of the English essay from its beginnings to 1700 and is co-authoring a study of Ben Jonson for the Twayne's English Authors Series.

Preface

This study of Owen Felltham attempts to further the growing reputation of an essayist and poet whose work has suffered undeserved neglect. Owen Felltham, popular and respected in his own day, is too much ignored in ours. Until recently, his work has been represented in only the most specialized anthologies of seventeenth-century prose and poetry, and so little has he been studied that the biographical notices of him that have appeared in print are frequently both inaccurate and incomplete. In addition, some of the critical statements made about his works have displayed an ignorance of its scope and depth.

The chapter that opens this study presents a brief but complete account of Felltham's life, taking into consideration all of the discoveries made since the article in the *Dictionary of National Biography* was written nearly ninety years ago. It also sketches the political and religious influences important to an understanding of the man and his work. The second chapter is a close study of Felltham's most famous and most important work, *Resolves: Divine, Morall, Politicall.* This collection of brief prose works, the composition of which occupied his vacant hours during several periods between 1623 and 1661, is examined in such a way as to show both its unity and its diversity. The Christian Stoicism and the liberal Anglicanism underlying the work receive attention; and the changes in genre, style, and tone that the collection underwent as it was added to and revised are illustrated and discussed at length.

A Brief Character of the Low-Countries, Felltham's humorous dissection of the Dutch, has a comparatively small but nonetheless important place in the canon of this seventeenth-century amateur of letters. The discussion of it here focuses on its relationship to its predecessors, its unique contribution to the character genre, the features of its style and humor, and its serious content.

Felltham's poems, praised highly in the seventeenth century and now almost completely ignored, are few in number; but several of them are significant works of art. Of special interest are the occasional poems written about literary, political, and religious subjects; the fine brief epitaphs; and the excellent love lyrics that show the mingling of a metaphysical stance with a classical simplicity of form, the best of John Donne and Ben Jonson. All of Felltham's poems are discussed in Chapter 4 of this study, the more important ones at some length.

The chapter on Felltham's reputation accomplishes two things: it surveys the alternating periods of praise and neglect that his works have undergone in the more than three centuries since they began to appear; and it attempts to place the poetry and prose in critical perspective, assigning to Felltham's works a defensible position alongside that of the best minor writers of his century.

In Chapters 2 and 3, I have quoted copiously from Felltham's works. I have done so because — with the exception of a few isolated resolves — his prose work is available only in large research libraries. A small portion of Chapter 2 was published, in somewhat different form, in *Publications of the Modern Language Association* (January 1972). Some of the critical assessments in Chapter 4 first appeared in *The Poems of Owen Felltham* (University Park, Pennsylvania: Seventeenth-Century News, 1973), which I co edited with Claude J. Summers.

Such a book as this present one could not have been written without much assistance, both institutional and individual. I should like to express my thanks to the Graduate School, the University of Illinois at Urbana, for the grant of a Faculty Summer Fellowship in 1967 that enabled me to check rare printed materials and unique manuscripts in England and in The Netherlands. In this connection, I should also like to thank Professor Robert B. Ogle, former Head of the English Department of the University of Illinois at Chicago Circle, for his encouragement and aid in the project. I wish to acknowledge the assistance of the administrators, librarians, and archivists at the Huntington Library, the British Museum, the Buckingham Palace Road branch of the Westminster Public Library, the Bodley Library, the Public Record Office, Somerset House, and the University Library, Amsterdam. For his general interest in the project and his willingness to read the typescript and offer suggestions, I am very grateful to my late friend Napier Wilt.

Two special debts deserve special attention. The late Donald Cor-

Preface

nu, Professor of English at the University of Washington, was generous over and beyond the dictates of professional courtesy. Although we never met, he not only gave me complete freedom to use the materials in his pioneering dissertation but also presented me with his personal, annotated copy of the 1661 edition of *Resolves*. Most of all, however, for the many long hours that he spent with the successive stages of the manuscript, offering innumerable valuable insights and suggestions, I owe an unpayable debt of gratitude to my colleague and friend Claude J. Summers, The University of Michigan — Dearborn.

TED-LARRY PEBWORTH

The University of Michigan — Dearborn

Acknowledgments

The quotations from *Resolves* are reproduced by permission of The Huntington Library, San Marino, California; those from *A Brief Character of the Low-Countries* by permission of the British Museum. The only editorial liberties taken are an expansion of printers' contractions and a regularization in the use of italics. The transcript of Felltham's will is the author's, made through the courtesy of Somerset House. The poetry is quoted from *The Poems of Owen Felltham*, edited by Ted-Larry Pebworth and Claude J. Summers (University Park, Pennsylvania: Seventeenth-Century News, 1973).

Chronology

1604(?)	Owen Felltham born, probably at Mutford, Suffolk.
1610 - 1623	Educated in the standard Latin authors, probably by a private tutor.
1623	Publishes *Resolues: Diuine, Morall, Politicall* (licensed 26 May), a collection of one hundred brief essays of a serious and pious nature.
1623 - 1628	Makes a three-week trip to Holland. Writes the humorous "A Brief Character of the Low-Countries under the States," but does not publish it. Writes occasional poems.
1628	Publishes a second edition of *Resolves*, to which are added one hundred longer essays, or "Excogitations," on various subjects. Also publishes a third edition this same year, reversing the order of the two parts.
1628 - 1647	Contributes a few occasional poems to various books. Goes to London where he meets Ben Jonson and Thomas Randolph. Appointed steward by Barnabas O'Brien (after 1639, the sixth Earl of Thomond). Probably takes charge of O'Brien's English property at Great Billing, Northamptonshire. Marries Mary Clopton of Kentwell Hall, Melford, Suffolk. Probably writes but does not publish his love lyrics. Allows some of his unpublished poems and "Low-Countries" to circulate in manuscript.
1631	Publishes a fourth edition of *Resolves*.
1634	Fifth edition of *Resolves*.
1636	Sixth edition of *Resolves*.
1647	Seventh edition of *Resolves*.
1647 - 1661	Revises the earlier one hundred essays of *Resolves;* enlarges some, discards some, and adds others. Probably during this time writes the two discourses, "Something upon Eccles. ii.11" and "upon St. Luke xiv.20." Writes,

but does not publish, several occasional poems, including "An Epitaph to the Eternal Memory of Charles the First. . . ."

1648 A pirated edition of "Low-Countries" issued under the title *Three Moneths Observations of the Low Countries, especially Holland.*

1652 A second edition of the pirated "Low-Countries" printed; a correct, but anonymous version issued by Henry Seile, the printer of *Resolves.*

1657 Barnabas O'Brien dies; Felltham continues in the service of his widow, the Dowager Countess Mary.

1659 A second edition of the authoritative version of *Low-Countries* published, again anonymously.

1660 A third authoritative, but anonymous printing of *Low-Countries.*

1661 An eighth edition of *Resolves* published with major revisions; to it appended the two discourses and *Lusoria, or Occasional Pieces,* consisting of forty-two poems, eighteen letters, and *Low-Countries.*

1661 - Writes "A Form of Prayer Compos'd for the Family of the
1668 Right Honorable the Countess of THOMOND."

1662 Another authoritative edition of *Low-Countries,* with Felltham's name on the title page.

1667/8 Dies February 23 at the London house of the Dowager Countess of Thomond. Buried the next day at St. Martin-in-the-Fields, Westminster.

CHAPTER 1

Owen Felltham, Gentleman

I His Life and Works

RELATIVELY few details are known about the life of Owen
Felltham.[1] Even the place and date of his birth are uncertain;
but it is likely that he was born at Mutford, a village near Lowestoft,
Suffolk, in 1604.[2] He was the second son of Thomas Felltham,[3] a
well-to-do member of the gentry, and his wife Mary, daughter of
John Ufflete, Gentleman, of Somerleyton, Suffolk. The Fellthams
had been important landowners in Norfolk and Suffolk for at least
three centuries before Owen's birth; records place the family at
Felltham's Manor, Norfolk, as early as the thirteenth century.
Owen's father was heir of the family and bore arms: on a field *sable*,
two bars *ermine*, in chief three leopards' faces *or*. Owen, who frequently affixed "Gentleman" to his name, was undoubtedly proud
of his family's position; the Felltham arms appear on the engraved
title pages of all the seventeenth-century editions of *Resolves* except
the first one.

Thomas and Mary Felltham had two other sons, Robert and
Thomas. Robert, who entered the legal profession, was for a time an
attorney of the Court of Chancery before settling in Sculthorpe, Norfolk. Thomas became a vintner in Norwich and grew wealthy. Both
were still living when Owen made his will in 1667. There were three
girls in the family. Mary and Elizabeth both married Suffolk men;[4]
Frances married a gentleman out of Yorkshire.[5] Since Felltham
makes no mention of his sisters in his will, they probably did not survive him.

Of the first eighteen years of Owen Felltham's life, nothing
definite is known. Although he was later to have a poem published in
Parnassus Biceps, a collection of verse by alumni of Oxford and
Cambridge, no record exists of his having attended either of these

universities. Judging from the first edition of *Resolves*, Felltham
very likely received the same kind of education that D. C. Allen
speculates for Sir William Cornwallis: "The nature of his linguistic
knowledge and the narrow limits of his reading indicate a man
whose education was in the hands of tutors. There is nothing to
suggest that he had been through the university curriculum. . . . My
feeling is that Cornwallis' education was squirearchical and that he
was, in a fashion, self-educated. His habit of quoting from adjacent
pages of the same book gives the impression that he was reading as
he wrote."[6] In the case of Owen Felltham, this self-education was a
life-long pleasure. He had read much by 1623; the pieces added to
Resolves in 1628 show an expanding list of authors, both secular and
divine, whose works had been read with profit; and by 1661, when
Resolves reached its final state, Felltham exhibits as much knowledge as any university man, and more discrimination and humanity
than most.

Although no date appears on the title page, the first edition of
Resolves: Divine, Morall, Politicall undoubtedly appeared in 1623.
Its author's name is given on the title page as "Owin Felltham."[7]
Because this little book is so handsomely and carefully printed, one
anonymous nineteenth-century reviewer likened it to "the pet work
of a well-to-do person,"[8] a description that fits it well. That same
reviewer speculated that, since the first edition of *Resolves* is
dedicated to the Lady Dorothy Crane, Felltham was probably employed at that time as secretary to her father, the Right Honorable
Sir Henry Hobart, Lord Chief Justice of the Common Pleas.[9] No
evidence exists to prove or disprove the speculation, although such
employment is certainly plausible. One of the few professions open
to gentlemen during this time was that of secretary to some
nobleman, and Felltham was later to spend above forty years in a
somewhat similar capacity to the Earls of Thomond.

Felltham's whereabouts between 1623 and 1628 is unknown, but
he probably made his three-week trip to Holland during this period.
From that journey came the inspiration for his rather lengthy
pamphlet *A Brief Character of the Low-Countries under the States*.
This lively work, probably written shortly after his tour, circulated
widely in manuscript and in pirated editions before being issued in
an authoritative edition in 1652. Felltham also began to write poetry
in the mid-1620s; and during the following thirty years, several of his
commendatory and elegiac poems appeared in print.

The second, expanded edition of *Resolves* was issued early in

1628, the new pieces in it dedicated to Thomas, Baron Coventry, Lord Keeper of the Great Seal. Felltham was not in London in 1627 or 1628 when this volume was being prepared for the press; on the errata page, the printer comments, "The Authors absence ha's made faults multiply." Felltham must have come to the capital shortly thereafter, however, at which time he met Ben Jonson and Jonson's young friend and literary protégé, Thomas Randolph. He also seems to have met about this time the flamboyant Sir Kenelm Digby and his beautiful wife Venetia, both friends of Jonson. During the next few years, Felltham was to write poems on these important figures.

At some time near the beginning of the 1630s, Felltham became steward to Barnabas O'Brien, a younger brother of the Irish fifth Earl of Thomond. Around 1628, O'Brien had purchased a manor at Great Billing, a village a few miles from Northampton; and Felltham probably lived there to oversee the property and to collect rents. In 1639, Barnabas succeeded to his brother's title of Earl of Thomond; in 1645, he was created Marquess of Billing by King Charles; but, since the patent did not pass under the Great Seal, he never assumed that title. In 1646, the Earl and Countess took up residence at Great Billing.[10] Felltham spent the rest of his life in the service of the O'Briens; when the sixth Earl died in 1657, he continued as steward under his son Henry, the seventh Earl, and the Dowager Countess Mary.[11]

Probably a short time after securing his position with the O'Briens, Felltham married Mary Clopton of Kentwell Hall, Melford, Suffolk, Of her, nothing further is known. In the 1661 *Resolves*, Felltham published a letter which he had written to her, addressing her as "Clarissa," along with two letters written to his mother-in-law, "Olivia." Mary Felltham probably died before her husband; no mention of her appears in his will. If they had any children, they also must have died before their father since the will contains no mention of any offspring.[12] Donald Cornu suggests that Felltham's love lyrics, published in the 1661 *Resolves*, were inspired by his wife and that, upon her death, probably at an early age, Felltham was so grieved that he determined not to remarry.[13]

In 1637 and 1638, Felltham exchanged letters with William Johnson, an Englishman at the Jesuit College in Cadiz. Johnson wrote to Felltham expressing admiration for some parts of *Resolves* but deploring Felltham's attitude toward Roman Catholicism. Felltham's answer, many times longer than Johnson's letter, upholds the position of the Church of England; and Felltham supports his argument with an impressive number of citations from Biblical and post-Biblical authority. Interestingly, he refutes Johnson's position by using Roman Catholic, particularly Jesuit, writers. Although Felltham maintained a lifelong and fervent interest in the Church, no evidence indicates that he took orders. He did have a collection of theological works, which he bequeathed to his nephew, Thomas Felltham, a minister; and he probably conducted family services for the Dowager Countess Mary. Two of his sermons or "discourses" survive, "Something upon Eccles. ii.11" and "upon St. Luke xiv.20," as does "A Form of Prayer Compos'd for the Family of the Right Honorable the Countess of THOMOND." Felltham probably occupied a position that now would be designated lay reader.

Felltham's whereabouts during the decade of the Civil War is uncertain, but he very likely remained at Great Billing. Northamptonshire was controlled by the Parliamentarians during most of the period of conflict. Felltham mentions the war in the 1661 *Resolves*, but he does not suggest that he was an active participant. Most of his time during the Interregnum was probably also spent at the O'Brien manor, overseeing the property, writing poetry, and revising the 1623 resolves. As evidenced by his essays "Of Conscience" and "Of Peace," published in the 1661 *Resolves*, Felltham was overjoyed at the Restoration. He happily concurred with Parliament in dating the reign of Charles II from 1649, the year that Charles I was executed. In his will, Felltham refers to 1667 as "the 19th yeare of the Raigne of our soueraigne Lord Charles the second. . . ."

In 1661, Felltham published what is obviously a collection of the works that he wished to be remembered by: the eighth edition of *Resolves*, to which he appended the two discourses on Biblical passages, forty-two poems, *A Brief Character of the Low-Countries*, and a sheaf of letters. The book, a handsome small folio, is dedicated in its entirety to the Dowager Countess of Thomond.

In his last years, Felltham divided his time between the Thomond seat at Great Billing and the Dowager Countess's townhouse in the Strand. The manor at Great Billing became a favorite of courtiers of Charles II; and on at least one occasion the Duke of York (later James II) was entertained there. Joseph Williamson, Latin Secretary in the early 1660s and Secretary of State from 1664 to 1667, and Edmund King, personal physician to Charles II, were frequent guests. These two men witnessed Felltham's last will and testament.

That document was prepared on 4 May 1667. By a happy chance, the original copy, written on two sheets of foolscap in Felltham's own hand, is still extant, preserved in the archives of Somerset House.[14] Besides being beautifully phrased, the will contains several passages of interest. It begins, as is usual with such documents in Felltham's day, by praising God and bequeathing to Him the testator's soul:

Glory bee to God on High On Earth Peace and Good Will towards men: I Owen Felltham of Great Billinge in the County of Northton being no way distempered with any disease or Infirmity to Cloud my vnderstandinge or Memory for which I giue God humble thanks, yett because the Life of Man is but as a wind that passeth away & is no more I doe heere by Gods permission make and Ordaine this My Last Will and Testament in Manner & forme followinge. First I do humbly Contentedly & thankfully resigne vp my Soule & Spirit to my Gratious & Omnipotent God (who first bestowed it on mee) whensoeuer he shall please to release mee from his Corruptible world vpon whose Infinite Goodnes & Mercy in the Mission Passion Resurrection Ascention & Intercession of his Blessed Sonne my Sauiour Jesus Christ I doe wholly & solely Relye for my Saluation disclaiminge totally all Meritt of my owne vnles it be of his most iust Indignation for my many Offences. being through the frailety & Corruption of humane Nature so far from deseruinge a Pardon for my Manifold Sinnes, That I doe not hold my selfe worthy to aske one. but doe wholly Cast my selfe vpon that Infinitely Noble & Incomprehensible Nature and Bounty of my God and Great Creator & Preseruer who vses not to faile those Humbled soules that trust him, nor to take delight in the smart & Punishment of his Creature But in doing it Good and Conferringe Felicity on it And heerin is my Trust & dependance in hope Hee will graciously Consider my frailety to haue mercy vpon mee.

This lengthy preamble is followed by instructions for his funeral:

For my Body where it shall fall to Earth I am Content that in that parish there the Trunke be laid. the sooner after my decease the better in the Church or any where, where my Executor pleases. with as little Ceremony as decently may bee. When the Jewell is gone wee use not to be solicitous about the Case aboue 30li. I would not haue bestowed to Bury mee And if my Executor please he may Cause this Annexed Inscription to be sett vp in ye wall neere the place where I shall be Interred[.]

The sum of thirty pounds seems modest enough today, but it was in Felltham's time an inordinate amount of money to spend on a funeral. The privilege of burial inside a church usually cost no more than five shillings, and other expenses connected with interment must have been proportionately low. Perhaps the bulk of the money allotted for funeral expenses Felltham intended to be spent on the inscribed tablet. The "Annexed Inscription" is missing from the copy of the will in Somerset House, but it was probably the Latin epitaph with which Felltham closes the 1661 *Resolves*. The church where Felltham was buried unfortunately was rebuilt in the early eighteenth century; and most of the memorial stones and plaques in the old edifice, including Felltham's, were broken up to serve as foundation materials for the new building.

Felltham designated his nephew and namesake, Owen Felltham of Gray's Inn, executor and gave him the lease to some Irish properties. The bequests in his will reveal that Felltham became rather wealthy in the service of the O'Briens. In addition to real estate and money, which he parceled out to various relatives and friends, Felltham made many small bequests. To his "kind friend," Anne Seile, publisher of the 1661 edition of *Resolves*, he left "tenne pownds to buy hir a piece of plate, whereby to remember me"; to his "Nephew Thomas Felltham minister," he left his library of Biblical commentary; and to his long-time employer and patroness, the Dowager Countess of Thomond, he left the price of a ring, "humbly beseeching hir that shee will Honor mee in accepting so small a remembrance of my thankfulnes wth my prayers for the Continuance of hir Life & Happines."

Owen Felltham died on February 23, 1667/8, at the London house of the Dowager Countess. The next day he was buried in St. Martin-in-the-Fields. His memorial tablet, if one was ever erected for him, probably read:

> Postquam vidisset rotantem Mundum,
>   Imaque summis supernatantia,
> Prosperum Tyrio scelus imbutum,
> Dum Virtus sordida squallet in Aula,
>   Securique cervicem praebuit:
>   Injusta tamen Hominum
>   In justissima disponente Deo;
> Dum Redux *Caesar* Nubila pellit,
> Gloriamque Gentis tollit in altum:
>   Tandem evadens Terris,
> Exuvias hic reliquit F E L L T H A M.[15]

> (Having seen in this spinning world
> That, though often rising to sit in state,
> Sin prospers, decking herself in purple,

> While Virtue, humbled, mourns in the courtyard
>   And presents her head to the axe;
>   The injustice of man is still
>   Redisposed most justly by God:
> Since the King, reinstated, banishes clouds
> And the nation's glory rises on high;
>   At last, escaping the earth,
> FELLTHAM leaves here his mortal remains.)

As is quite evident from his epitaph, Felltham's life was profoundly influenced by the interconnected political and religious controversies of his day — as was most of what he wrote.

II   *The Political and Religious Climate of His Time*

Owen Felltham was born at the beginning of a new era in England. The old queen was dead; and a new, Scottish monarch sat on the throne. Elizabeth had, during her long reign (1558 - 1603), steered a politically wise course between extremes. Her Northern cousins James I and his son Charles I were unable or unwilling to do the same, and the first two-thirds of the seventeenth century was a period of political and religious turmoil.

The great Elizabethan "compromise" had been, in a real sense, both political and religious. Falling heir to religious upheaval, Elizabeth set herself the task of establishing a state church which would be acceptable to all but the most unreformable Roman Catholics in her kingdom. With the aid of very capable advisors, she reestablished a Church of England, but one considerably different from that which had existed under her father and her younger brother. Theirs had been essentially a conservative church, the Roman Catholic faith divested of a Pope, but otherwise almost intact. The liturgy was, of course, in English, but it was to all intents and purposes the Roman liturgy; and the major tenets of the faith likewise remained unchanged.

As a result of the religious persecutions during the reign of Queen Mary (1553 - 1558), however, a new element had entered the spiritual life of England: the continental Protestantism of John Calvin. Refugee English priests who refused to reenter the Roman communion at Queen Mary's order were welcomed at Geneva, and when they could safely return to England — Protestant once more under Elizabeth — they brought with them new and divisive doctrines: Election, Predestination, limited Grace. And partner to these doctrines was a zeal to "purify" the Church of all traces of the corrupting ritual and custom with which generations of Popery had virtually smothered the true, "primitive" Church. These English Puritans, though few in number during the latter half of the sixteenth century, were a vocal group; and some of them attained positions of importance in the Established Church.

Queen Elizabeth, as "Supreme Governor" of the Church of England, had to satisfy both conservative English Christians — those who would later be referred to as the High Church or Anglo-Catholic party — and the new Puritans. The instrument of compromise, which achieved the grudging acceptance of both sides, was the Articles of Religion, thirty-nine statements of belief and practice to which all clergy had to subscribe. Most of the articles concerned matters over which there was no dispute. Those which did treat of contentious subjects such as Election, Predestination, Free Will, and Good Works were purposely worded in a vague fashion, allowing each Englishman to interpret their meaning as he wished.

Throughout her reign, Elizabeth refused to be drawn into public controversy concerning her Church. As long as Englishmen accepted and practiced the outward forms of the Church of England, their private beliefs were of little or no consequence. And the Puritan element, though dissatisfied at not having obtained complete control of the Establishment, was not rash enough to defy with force the Queen and her episcopacy.

The other dispute which might have caused serious trouble during Elizabeth's reign was that concerning the relative powers and spheres of control exercised by the monarch and her parliaments. In the sixteenth century, England began to send wealthy and intelligent men to the House of Commons. Many of these were shrewd, self-made men; and some began to feel, and to express, resentment that their legislative powers were so few. Commons sought to enlarge its role in the government, and it discovered that its most important leverage came from its control over taxation. Only Parliament could levy major taxes. Elizabeth was able, at times through little more than the strength of her personality, to hold on to her hereditary rights in the face of Parliament's encroachment. To avoid compromising her prerogatives, she managed by selling Crown lands and by borrowing large sums of money to evade Parliamentary control. Through a combination of tact, personal force, and debt she kept her government stable; and most Englishmen, living better than they ever had before, did not question her right to rule almost absolutely.

King James I, who reigned in England from 1603 to 1625, had been since infancy King James VI of Presbyterian Scotland. His accession to the English throne naturally gave English Puritans hope that they would have a chance to rid the Established Church of episcopacy and Popery. But the new King had other ideas. He was willing to compromise somewhat on religious matters. He did attempt to correct the most serious abuses in the Church, agreeing with the Puritans that episcopal pluralism should cease, that the clergy should be made up of educated men, and that the power of excommunication should belong to only the major clergy. But James was very jealous of his powers. He determined to rule, by Divine Right, as absolute monarch of his new kingdom; and he saw in the Puritan demand that episcopacy be abolished the first step toward democratizing the government. His fear was expressed in his famous comment, "No bishops, no king." Although the Puritans began to take over the House of Commons during James I's reign, the King was able to avoid undue conflict with his parliaments.

The reign of his son, Charles I (1625 - 1649), saw the political-religious conflicts of the kingdom culminate in civil war. Charles favored more catholicism, not less, in the Established Church; and he selected William Laud, a sincere though tactless High Churchman, to be Archbishop of Canterbury. Charles had much more trouble with Parliament than his father had. The first four parliaments called during his reign insisted on Puritan reform of the Church and refused to vote the King the taxation that he needed to run the government. Finally, his fifth Parliament (called in 1640) determined to make itself the supreme ruler of England. In the thirteen years that it sat, Commons declared war on Charles I (1642), executed Archbishop Laud (1644), and at Oliver Cromwell's insistence set up a commission which tried the King for treason and ordered his execution (1649).

During the 1640s, the Puritans disputed among themselves. Some were Presbyterian and wished a synod form of church government; some were Independents, declaring that each congregation should be allowed to define its own creed and ritual. Under the leadership of Cromwell, the Independents gained control of government and Church. Episcopacy was dissolved, and ritualism was abolished.

England was without a monarch for eleven years (1649 - 1660). During most of that time, Oliver Cromwell was in control of the nation and ruled effectively. His genius did not extend to his eldest son, however, and a Cromwellian dynasty did not materialize. When

Oliver Cromwell died (1658), his son Richard assumed the position of Lord Protector, but was unable to hold the government together. Finally, in 1660, England sent for the exiled Charles II, eldest son of Charles I. The monarchy and the Church of England were restored, and — for a decade at least — there was stability once more.

As will become clear in the following pages, the literary efforts of Owen Felltham reflect closely the times in which they were written. The poetry and prose of his young manhood are filled with apprehension caused in large part by the emerging divisiveness in church and state; the poems of his middle years reflect mixed anger and sorrow over civil war, political execution, and Puritan repression; the works of his last years exhibit the great joy with which he viewed the Restoration. Other intellectual and emotional trends also influenced Felltham's literary efforts. They, along with the stylistic models which shaped his prose and poetry, are considered in the following discussions of his individual works.

CHAPTER 2

Resolves: Divine, Morall, Polticall

O WEN Felltham is remembered primarily as the author of a single important work — a collection of prose pieces issued originally in 1623 as *Resolues: Diuine, Morall, Politicall* and extensively enlarged and revised during the following thirty-eight years. The work appeared during those years in eight editions, or "impressions" as some of the title pages misleadingly claim; and these eight editions represent four distinct stages in the growth of the whole collection. The first edition, licensed for publication on 26 May 1623, was issued by the stationer Henry Seile whose shop was "at the Tygers head in St Paules Churchyard" in London. Seile himself published the first seven editions of *Resolves*, and his widow Anne issued the eighth.

The first edition is a small duodecimo containing one hundred brief and untitled prose works (hereafter referred to as the "Short Century" and abbreviated "S."); these pieces are properly described as "resolves." The book is dedicated to the Lady Dorothy Crane, daughter of Lord Hobart, Chief Justice of the Common Pleas. Five years later, the work was enlarged and reissued in quarto with the title *Resolves A Duple Century one new an other of a second Edition* (1628A). To the original one hundred resolves are added a second "century" (hereafter referred to as the "Long Century" and abbreviated "L."); these pieces are designated by Felltham as "excogitations." Although critics and literary historians often discuss these Long Century pieces in terms of the personal essay, these excogitations actually show close kinship to the meditation. These new works, each bearing a title, are paged separately from the original resolves and are dedicated to Thomas, Lord Coventry, Baron of Alesborough, Lord Keeper of the Great Seal.

In the third edition of *Resolves* (1628B), a hastily and poorly printed quarto, the author changes the order of the two parts of his

book and supplies titles for the original short pieces. The fourth
through the seventh editions of *Resolves* (1631, 1634, 1636, and
1647) follow the text and the format of the third edition, and all are
poorly printed quartos. The eighth edition of the book (1661), the
last published during Felltham's lifetime, is a handsome small folio,
dedicated in its entirety to Mary, Dowager Countess of Thomond.
This edition incorporates major revisions. The Long Century of 1628
is retained intact; the Short Century of 1623 is replaced by eighty-
five lengthy personal essays (hereafter referred to as the "Revised
Short Century" and abbreviated "R. S."). Sixty-two of these are
revisions of resolves in the original century; the other twenty-three
are wholly new pieces. Also in this publication, but paged separately
from *Resolves*, is a collection of poetry and prose entitled *Lusoria*. In
this form, Felltham's book was reissued three more times before the
turn of the century (1670, 1677, and 1696) and again in 1709.

I   *The Cumulative Effect of* Resolves

In its totality, *Resolves: Divine, Morall, Politicall* is a collection of
two hundred eighty-five short prose works of various kinds.[1] Subjects
discussed in the book are almost as numerous as the essays themselves, and the pieces — each of which may be read independently
of the others — are arranged in no thematic order. *Resolves* obviously is not a book to be read from beginning to end; instead, it is
one "to be tasted." In fact, since the essays are not grouped according to subject matter, several of the early editions have large
"Alphabetical Tables," or indices, attached to aid the systematic
reader.

Even a very brief list of the titles shows something of the varied
contents: "The Misery of being Old and ignorant" (S. 38), "Gouernment and Obedience the two causes of a Common Prosperitie" (S.
53), "A good Rule in wearing of Apparell" (S. 58), "To reuenge
wrongs, what it sauours of" (S. 84), "Of the vncertainety of life" (L.
32), "Of Dreames" (L. 52), "Of the Soule" (L. 64), "Of Scandall"
(L. 91), "Of the Salvation of the Heathen" (R. S. 19), "Of Distrust
and Credulity" (R. S. 42), "Of the use of Pleasure" (R. S. 50), "Of
Dancing" (R. S. 70). Yet despite the thirty-eight-year period covered
in the composition, the independent nature of each essay, and the
great variety of subject matter, *Resolves: Divine, Morall, Politicall*
emerges as a unified work; it is held together by the didactic purpose
inherent in all the essays and by the personality of its author.

Resolves is designed to aid Felltham and its readers in their quest for the good life. In "To the Reader," prefaced to the 1661 edition, either the printer or Felltham himself (writing in the third person) echoes Michel de Montaigne *(Essaies* I.54) in indicating the audience toward which the pieces are directed: ". . . They were written to the middle sort of people. For the wisest, they are not high enough; nor yet so flat and low, as to be only fit for fools: whosoever pleaseth only these, is miserable." Quoting Cicero, the writer of the preface concludes: "Too profound, or too shallow, he holds not proportionate to the Work." *Resolves* was, then, designed neither for philosophers or theologians, nor for the unthinking mob, but for members of the great squirearchical and merchant classes: in short, the work was for people very much like Felltham himself. Although few of these persons were university educated, nearly all were vitally interested in the practical problems which confronted the Christian in seventeenth-century England.

The resolves, to a greater or lesser degree, concern the private virtues — the human being's proper attitude toward his God and toward himself — and the public ones — man's best approach to his fellows and to the world at large. As the complete title of his book indicates, Felltham writes on matters divine (spiritual questions and points of doctrine), moral (ethical problems which are more properly the province of philosophy than of theology), and political (the question of government in particular and all human intercourse in general). The approach and purpose of *Resolves* are clearly indicated in the engraved allegorical title pages of the book's seventeenth-century editions. One design, used only for the 1623 edition, combines representations of worldly commerce with the Stoic virtues of constancy and fortitude and the Christian aids of faith, the law, the evangelists, and the crucifixion; and the whole is focused on prudence, innocence, love, friends, and God. The motto, adapted appropriately from Horace's defense of his modest station and simple life *(Satires,* I. vi), is "His [sic] ego Commodius, quam tu præclare Senator millibus atque alijs viuo" (By these and a thousand others I live in more comfort than you, famous senator).

The other design, used in the second and subsequent editions of *Resolves,* has at its apex the ineffable name of God, toward which rises a winged heart. Beneath the heart, the arms of wisdom and truth support the universe in the form of a globe. Two women, representing worldly opinion and ignorance, pull the universe downward with ropes of vanity. The motto, "et sic demulceo Vitam" (and thus I smooth out life), reflects the Stoic Christian nature of the

book. Beginning with the third edition of *Resolves*, this allegorical
design is accompanied by Felltham's versified explanation of it,
"*The Face of the Book*, Unmasked":

> Here, th'*Universe* in Natures Frame,
> Sustain'd by *Truth*, and *Wisdomes* hand,
> Does, by *Opinions* empty Name,
> And *Ignorance*, distracted stand:
> Who with strong *Cords* of vanity, conspire,
> Tangling the *Totall*, with abstruse Desire.
>
> But then the *Noble Heart* infir'd,
> With *Rayes*, divinely from above,
> Mounts (though with wings moist and bemir'd)
> The great *Gods glorious Light* to prove,
> Slighting the World: yet selfrenouncing, tries,
> That where *God* draws not, there she sinks, and dies.

Felltham also makes clear the didactic purpose of *Resolves* in the
prefatory remarks in various editions of the book. In the "Epistle
Dedicatorie" of 1623, addressed to the Lady Dorothy Crane, he
writes: "If euer Resolutions were needful, I thinke they be in this
Age of loosenesse. . . ." In the note "To the Peruser" in the same
edition, Felltham states his reason for writing his own body of
resolutions: "What I aime at in it, I confesse, hath most respect to
my selfe: That I might out of my owne Schoole take a lesson, should
serue mee for my whole Pilgrimage: and if I should wander from
these rests, that my owne Items might set me in heuens direct way
againe."

In a recent study of *Resolves*, McCrea Hazlett credits too much
Felltham's assertion that he wrote the Short Century of *Resolves* entirely for his own private use.[2] A standard statement in all prefaces
and epistles dedicatory to works written by gentlemen authors in the
seventeenth century was a disavowal that the works then published
were written for publication. Hardly anyone, however, takes these
disavowals seriously. Felltham was a very young man, eighteen or
nineteen years old, when *Resolves* was published in 1623; and he
could have had at that time little literary reputation. If he had not
actively solicited the publication of his first efforts at authorship, the
book quite likely would not have been published so soon after its
composition as it was. While it is true that Felltham seems in these
early resolves to be writing primarily to himself, the implication is

strong that he intends, or at least hopes, that others will follow his "Pilgrimage." And one cannot deny the hortatory quality of the Long and Revised Short Centuries. Although *Resolves* is a didactic book, intended as a guide in the pursuit of the Christian life, it is certainly not a dull one. In his wise appreciation of *Resolves*, Douglas Bush succinctly characterizes Felltham's ability to be at the same time pious and interesting: "Although he seeks the *via media* in all things — except the love of God and hatred of evil — and although the commonplaces of religion and morals are his staple article, he can, more than most didactic essayists, make virtue sound exciting and moderation adventurous."[3]

The various stages through which *Resolves* passed during Felltham's lifetime saw a shift in genre from the resolve formula of 1623 to the personal essay of 1661. The style also shifts from the Senecan aphorism of 1623 to the more nearly conversational prose of 1661. As the book developed, there were elaborations of content and changes in attitude; but, as a whole, Felltham's world view and his basic beliefs remained constant; and what emerges from an examination of all the stages of *Resolves* is the picture of an attractive and interesting human being who is very much a man of his own time.

Felltham's world view is conservative. Even though he began writing some years after the emergence of the New Science,[4] he shows in *Resolves* a preference for the old order, the Ptolemaic universe as Christianized during the middle ages. The mutable, corruptible earth is at the center of the universe; encasing it, sphere within sphere, the immutable, incorruptible planets move in their appointed paths; and these planets are enclosed in turn by the fixed stars and governed in their movements by the *primum mobile*, that is, by God in the person of the "first mover." This concept of the universe teaches Felltham that "order and degree" are of paramount importance in questions divine, moral, or political. Everyone and everything, from the angels to the lowest clods of earth, have their appointed places in the Chain of Being. One of man's chief tasks in life is to find his appropriate place and then, often a more difficult task, to make himself content with it. Sin is, basically, the revolt of man against God's order. Felltham's resolve, "The great Good of Good Order" (S. 81), is as concise a prose statement of the concepts of the Ptolemaic universe, the Chain of Being, and Order and Degree as can be found in seventeenth-century English literature.

This fervent desire for order in all things leads naturally, at least in Felltham's case, to a reliance on the monarch (God's order as it

manifests itself in political affairs) and on the Established Church
(God's order in religious matters). And it makes Felltham strive for
order in his own life, manifesting itself in an emphasis on moderation. In "How hee must liue, that liues well" (L. 100), Felltham
reflects the interdependence of order in the individual's life and in
the affairs of state: "For our selues; wee need order; for our
neighbour, Charity; and for our God, our Reuerence, and Humility:
and these are so certainly linked one to another, as he that liues
orderly, cannot but bee acceptable, both to God, and the world.
Nothing iarres the worlds Harmony, like men that breake their
rankes. One turbulent Spirit will dissentiate even the calmest
kingdome. Wee may see the beauty of order, in nothing more, then
in some princely Procession. . . ." And in "Of Puritans" (L. 5), he
sees the Separatist as "a Church-Rebell, or one that would exclude
order. . . ." In "How to establish a troubled Gouernment" (S. 15),
Felltham compares himself to a state — the microcosm-macrocosm
analogy so popular in the Renaissance — and argues for moderation,
holding in check the bestial elements in himself: "My passions, and
affections are the chiefe disturbers of my Ciuill State: What peace
can I expect within mee, while these Rebels rest vnouercome? If
they get a head, my Kingdome is diuided, so it cannot stand." On a
more mundane level, he warns himself to talk in moderation (S. 8,
"Of Silence. Of Babbling").

Though Felltham is a conservative in his world view, he is a liberal
in theology. For him, the Church of England is the great *via media*,
the moderate path between the extremes of Papacy and Puritanism.
As is obvious from the frequency with which he indicates his personal relationship with God and Christ, Felltham feels no absolute
need for a church which is an intercessor between man and the
Divine: " 'Tis a hard thing among men of inferiour ranke, to speake
to an earthly Prince: no King keepes a Court so open, as to giue ad-
mittance to all commers. . . . Oh how happy, how priuiledged is then
a Christian? who though he often liues heere in a slight esteeme,
yet can he freely conferre with the King of Heauen, who not onely
heares his intreaties, but delights in his requests, inuites him to
come, and promiseth a happy welcome; which he shewes in fulfilling his desires, or better, fitter for him" (S. 9, "Of Prayer").

Indeed, Felltham sees no absolute need for a church at all since
God may be seen in nature and in the human conscience, as well as
in the Bible: "GOD hath left three books to the world, in each of
which hee may easily be found: The Booke of the *Creatures*, the
book of *Conscience,* & his written *Word*. The first shewes his om-

nipotency. The second his Iustice: the third his mercy and goodnesse" (S. 68, "The three bookes, in which God may bee easily
found"). Further, in "Of the Salvation of the Heathen" (R. S. 19),
Felltham asserts that any good act and any real repentance after a
sinful act are acceptable worship of God, whether or not the person
performing the good act or repenting the sinful one has a knowledge
of Christ and His Church. Felltham does, however, believe that a
man more easily performs good acts and repents evil acts if he is a
Christian.

Although Felltham frequently uses terms often associated with
Calvinism — Election and Grace — his definitions are at odds with
John Calvin's. According to the Calvinists (among whom most of the
English Puritans numbered themselves), all men, through the sin of
Adam, are deserving of damnation. Before mankind was even
created, however, a prescient God decided to set aside some men for
salvation: the Elect. They are saved not through their merits or
beliefs but through God's arbitrary gift of Grace to them. Felltham
regards the manifestation of Grace not as God's gift of salvation to
the few but as the offer of salvation to all — an offer made manifest
in Christ's sacrifice. The Elect are those people who have the advantage of the Church in their quest for everlasting life: all Christians,
and not just a select few, are the beneficiaries of Grace. Since
Felltham can see goodness in even the heathen and since his God
offers salvation to all men, the Christianity of *Resolves* is a tolerant
and attractive one.

In *Resolves*, Felltham shows himself very much aware of evil in
the world. The fact that the good are often afflicted with poverty and
with the contempt of humanity while the evil are rewarded with
riches and the world's esteem particularly disturbs him: "I obserue
none more lyable to the world's false censure, then the vpright
nature, that is honest, and free" (S. 85, "Who is most subiect to Censure"). As a consequence of this uneasiness, Felltham turns to a
religious philosophy which enjoyed some popularity in his time,
Christian Stoicism. A revival of Stoic thought late in the sixteenth
century was led on the Continent by Justus Lipsius who, with others,
wedded the pagan Stoicism of such philosophers as Epictetus and
Seneca to the Old Testament Stoicism of Ecclesiastes and Job and to
such New Testament manifestations of the philosophy as the opening two chapters of St. Paul's first epistle to the Corinthians. The
result was to color much of European religious thinking for the next
two centuries.

Christian Stoicism was popularized in England by Felltham's

early mentor, Bishop Joseph Hall, often called the "English Senec." Hall's *Meditations and Vowes, Divine and Moral* (1606, 1609) had a great influence on Felltham's *Resolves*. The basic idea of Christian Stoicism is that, since on earth good is punished and evil is rewarded, the good man should fortify himself against pains and insults of the world and be secure in the belief that all would be set right at the Last Judgment, when rewards and punishments would be dealt out appropriately. In "Of being the World's Favourite without Grace" (S. 18), Felltham writes: "He that gets heauen, hath plenty enough; though the earth scornes to allow him any thing: he that failes of that, is truely miserable; though shee giue him all shee hath. Heauen without earth is perfect. Earth without Heauen is but a little more cheerly hell."

Felltham reflects his Christian Stoicism in two major ways. He quotes frequently, especially in the Long Century, the writings of Seneca and the books of Ecclesiastes and Job. And throughout all of *Resolves*, whole essays are often devoted to Stoic contemplations: "Humanitie and Miserie, are Parallels" (S. 19), "The vanitie and shortnesse of mans Life" (S. 57), "Of the vncertainety of life" (L. 32), "Of Preparing against Death" (R. S. 5). Although *Resolves* mirrors Felltham's Christian Stoicism, the book is by no means bleak. As Douglas Bush perceptively comments, "Felltham's harmony of Christianity and Stoicism is tempered and sweetened by a love of life and literature, by philosophic charity and undogmatic good sense."[5] These attractive aspects of Felltham's personality are everywhere present in *Resolves*. His love of life is reflected in the 1628 meditation "Of Puritans" (L. 5), in which he chides the overly pious for their constant seriousness by remarking that, within the bounds of moderation, man should enjoy this life as much as possible: "If mirth and recreations bee lawfull, sure such a one may lawfully vse it. If Wine were giuen to cheere the heart, why should I feare to vse it for that end? Surely, the merry soule is freer from intended mischiefe, then the thoughtfull man."

This last remark, perhaps echoing Caesar's comment about Cassius (*Julius Caesar*, I, ii, 192 - 95), is followed by one of Felltham's best and most frequently quoted aphorisms: "A bounded mirth, is a Pattent adding time and happines to the crazed life of Man." A key word in this statement is, of course, the adjective "bounded," which reflects the ancient dictum of nothing in excess; nevertheless, the emphasis is on "mirth." Illustrating pleasant aspects of life which the Christian may legitimately enjoy, Felltham, arguing from Biblical authority, expresses the concept of God as the perfect father:

God delights in nothing more, then in a cheerefull heart, carefull to performe him seruice. What Parent is it, that reioyceth not to see his Child pleasant, in the limits of a filiall duty? I know wee reade of Christs weeping, not of his laughter: yet wee see, hee graceth a Feast with his first Miracle; and that a Feast of ioy: And can we thinke that such a meeting could passe without the noise of laughter? What a lumpe of quickened care is the melancholike man? Change anger into mirth, and the Precept will hold good still: *Bee merry, but sinne not.*

Felltham then draws the portrait of what he considers an admirable and happy man: "A man that submits to reuerent Order, that sometimes vnbends himselfe in a moderate relaxation; and in all, labours to approue himselfe, in the serenenesse of a healthful Conscience. . . ." Certainly Felltham enjoyed dancing (R. S. 70, "Of Dancing") and the theater (L. 20, "Of Preaching" and R. S. 61, "Of Improving by good Examples") when each eschewed lewdness. And in the 1661 essay "Of the use of Pleasure" (R. S. 50), he defends all pleasures "legitimated by the bounty of Heaven" by remarking that ". . . God would never have instincted the appetition of pleasure, and the faculties of enjoying it, so strongly in the composure of Man, if he had not meant, that in decency he should make use of them. . . ."

Felltham found great pleasure in reading. The numerous quotations and allusions found in all three centuries of *Resolves* attest to the fact that he read widely and often liked what he read well enough to note passages for inclusion in his own essays. He also wrote perceptively about literature in "Of Idle Bookes" (S. 1 and R. S. 1), "A Rule in reading Authors" (S. 27), "Of Poets and Poetrie" (L. 70), and "Of reading Authors" (R. S. 27). Yet Felltham clearly "upholds wisdom and the amateur ideal of culture against mere knowledge and pedantry."[6] His good sense tells him that

you shall scarce find a more Foole, then sometimes a meere Scholler. He will speake *Greeke* to an Ostler, and *Latine* familiarly, to women that vnderstand it not. Knowledge is the treasure of the mind; But Discretion is the key: without which, it lyes dead, in the dulnesse of a fruitlesse rest. The practique part of Wisedome, is the best. A native ingenuity, is beyond the watchings of industrious study. . . . Men . . . conversing onely among bookes, are put into affectation, and pedantisme. . . . Company and Conversation are the best

Instructors for a Noble behaviour. And this is not found in a melancholy study alone. . . . So farre I will honour Knowledge, as to thinke, this art of the braine, when it meetes with able Nature in the minde, then onely makes a man compleat. (L. 44, "Of Wisdome and Science")

Despite admonitions everywhere in *Resolves* to avoid evil men, Felltham stresses equally the necessity for charity toward those who have succumbed to the world's temptations. Possibly alluding to the case of Sir Francis Bacon, who in 1621 was convicted of bribery and removed from his position as Lord Chancellor, Felltham writes in the 1623 resolve "Of Libelling against them that are falne" (S. 56): "I wonder what spirit they are indued withall, that can basely libell at a man that is falne! . . . To inuenome a name by libells, that already is openly tainted, is to adde stripes with an Iron rod, to one that is flayed with whipping: and is sure in a mind well-tempered, thought inhumane, diabolicall." When he revised this resolve thirty-eight years later, Felltham enlarged upon the subject of charity:

as 'tis hard, to find any man free from all that may merit reproof; so, 'tis as easie, in the best, to find something that we may reprehend. Yet, sure I am, Charity will rather abate the score, then inflame the reckoning. He that Libels transgresses against the common rule of Morality and Religion: he does not doe, as he would be done by. We ought rather to bemone the unfortunate, then unworthily to insult against him, . . . 'Tis a disposition quite unchristian, that we show in such bad actions, being wholly contrary to that intermutual amity and friendliness that should be in the world. . . . If men were heavenly, they would be enkindled with a warming fire of Love and Charity. . . . (R. S. 51, "Of Libelling")

And in "How hee must liue, that liues well" (L. 100), Felltham puts charity toward one's fellow man on the same level as reverence toward God.

Felltham's undogmatic good sense humanizes his religious zeal. In "To Perfection, what is most necessary" (S. 3), he warns that religion which does not make allowances for human nature "will seeme too hard," and it will be "feared, but not loued." In "That a wise man may gaine by any company" (L. 12), he asserts the independence of his good sense: "Hee that liues alwayes by Booke-rules, shall shew himselfe affected, and a Foole. I will doe that which I see comely, (so it bee not dishonest) rather then what a graue Philosopher commands mee to the contrarie. I will take, what I see is fitly good, from any; but I thinke there was neuer any one man, that

liu'd to be a perfect guide of perfection." If Felltham had been in-
clined to let his piety and his learning overrule his humanity,
Resolves: Divine, Morall, Politicall would be a collection of precepts
too idealistic to follow and too dry to read. But such an inclination
seems not to have been in him; and *Resolves* — though didactic —
unfolds as a warm human document, the reflection of an attractive
personality.

A composite picture of the man and his book may be somewhat
misleading, however, as it tends to give the impression that Felltham
underwent no spiritual or intellectual growth between his eighteenth
and his fifty-sixth years and that the pieces of the Revised Short Century are indistinguishable from those of the Short Century. Quite to
the contrary, the progressive stages of *Resolves* mirror their author's
maturation in both spirit and intellect. In addition, three interrelated
elements of the work — genre, style, and tone — change as the
author added to and revised the essays of the original edition. A
chronological examination of the progressive stages of *Resolves* il-
lustrates these changes.[7]

II   *The Resolves of the Short Century (1623)*

The youthful Owen Felltham, seeing much immorality in the lives
of his elders and recognizing within himself some inclination toward
sin, began his literary career with the publication of a "century" of
short prose works that were designed to serve as guideposts to
heaven. The genre he found congenial to such a purpose was the
resolve, a restrictive form of religious essay devised and popularized
by clerical writers during the Jacobean period.

The resolve and the vow, its close relative, developed out of the
concluding statements of religious meditations, but they soon
overshadowed the meditations to which they were attached. In his
Meditations and Vowes, Divine and Moral (1606; enlarged edition,
1609), Bishop Joseph Hall asserts that a meditation which stops short
of "an issue" — a conclusion designed to better the life and conduct
of the person meditating — is of little worth: "In Meditation, those,
which begin heavenly thoughts and prosecute them not, are like
those, which kindle a fire under green wood, and leave it as soon as it
but begins to flame; losing the hope of a good beginning, for want of
seconding it with a suitable proceeding. When I set myself to
meditate, I will not give over, till I come to an issue. It hath been
said by some, that the beginning is as much as the midst; yea, more
than all: but I say, the ending is more than the beginning."[8]

In Hall's collection, the meditation — though usually much longer than the attached vow — ceases to have an existence for its own sake and functions primarily as the contemplative prologue to the vow, which is a one- or two-sentence promise to God concerning future conduct. Hall's *Meditations and Vowes* were followed in 1614 by the collection *New Essayes: Meditations and Vowes*, written by the clergyman Thomas Tuke, and in 1620 by *Sundry Christian Resolves*, occasionally attributed to the prolific Richard Braithwait.[9] The 1623 resolves of Owen Felltham are in this line of development.

With two modifications, Felltham adopts in the Short Century the formula employed by Bishop Hall in *Meditations and Vowes*. Each piece begins with the brief statement of a religious, moral, or (Felltham adds) political proposition. The central portion is devoted to a meditation on that proposition which proves its truth and considers one or more of its ramifications; these meditations vary greatly in length in both Hall and Felltham. The piece concludes with an application of the religious, moral, or political truth to the author's own life and conduct; and this conclusion is the one- or two-sentence statement which is Hall's "vow" and Felltham's "resolve." Felltham's expansion of an essentially religious genre to include political subjects does not represent a major change in the form since he relates all human conduct ultimately to questions of religion or ethics; and his decision to "resolve" rather than to "vow" is explained in the last piece of the 1623 collection: "Resolutions may often change; sometimes for the better; and the last euer stands firmest. But vowes well made, should know no variance: For the first should bee sure, without alteration. Hee that violates their performance, failes in his duty: and euery breach is a wound to the soule. I will resolue oft, before I vow once; neuer resolue to vow, but what I may keep; neuer vow, but what I both can, and will keepe" (S. 100, "Though Resolutions change, yet Vowes should know no Varietie"). The vow is absolute, the resolve is tentative.

Though similar in pattern, the individual resolves of 1623 vary greatly in length; and the variation depends solely on the extent of the meditative section. One of the briefest is S. 100 which has been quoted in its entirety above. In it the proposition is a two-sentence statement distinguishing between vows and resolves; and the resolve is a tripartite series of proposed actions. The only element in it that might be considered meditative is the sentence which relates the consequences of a failure to keep a vow.

At the other extreme is S. 81, "The great Good of Good Order," in which the meditative portion is nine times longer than the proposition and the resolve combined. In it Felltham proposes: "Euen from naturall reason, is the wicked man prou'd to be sonne vnto Satan, and heire of hell, and torments"; and he resolves: "I will first order my minde by good resolution; then keepe it so, by a strong constancie." In between the proposition and the resolve, he meditates on the "glorious order" of the heavens ("the Sun hath his appointed circuit, the Moone her constant change, and euery Planet & Starre their proper course and place") and on the necessary reflection of that order in the society of man ("In this world, Order is the life of Kingdoms, Honours, Arts: and by the excellency of it, all things flourish and thriue"). He contrasts order with chaos: "Onely in hell is confusion, horrour, and amazing disorder. From whence the wicked man shewes himself sprung, for there is nothing that like him, liues so irregular, and out of compasse. Disorder is a bird of the Diuels hatching. . . ."

In a topical reference, he obliquely condemns as disorderly those Puritans who object to Anglican liturgy and who deny episcopal authority: ". . . I feare lest those that rent the Church for *Ceremonie*, haue some affinitie with that prince of mis-rule: wee oft finde the parents disposition, though not propagated to the child, yet followed by him. I do not censure, but doubt. We haue seldome knowne him good, that refuseth to obey good orders." And finally, providing a transition between the meditation and the resolve that follows it, Felltham concludes that, although perfect order is impossible in a post-Fall world, the striving toward such order as is possible should be of primary consideration in man's life: "things vncapable of a true forme, are euer mending: yet euer vnperfect: when the rankes are broken, the victory is in hazzard. One bad voice, can put twenty good ones out of tune." Despite its relatively great length, "The great Good of Good Order" is deliberately shaped according to Felltham's resolve formula, and thus it finally directs the meditation inward.

Some critics have seen little difference between Felltham's early resolves and the prose characters that were written in the early seventeenth century.[10] Although Felltham was well aware of the character — and indeed wrote an innovative work in the genre, *A Brief Character of the Low-Countries* — that form exerted only a minor influence on his 1623 resolves. The character dates from the fourth century B. C., when the Athenian philosopher Theophrastus published thirty short descriptions of types of unattractive persons who were controlled by "vices" or excesses of various kinds: greed, petty pride, boorishness, and the like. After lying dormant for centuries, the genre was repopularized in Europe by Isaac Casaubon's 1592 translation of Theophrastus, and it influenced to a considerable extent the emerging essay. Bishop Joseph Hall, again a pioneer, wrote the first English characters. He extended the range of the form to cover virtuous types and published *Characters of Vertues and Vices* in 1608. Hall's efforts were followed rather quickly by those of Sir Thomas Overbury, Thomas Dekker, John Webster, and even John Donne. In English hands, the character became a witty picture of a virtuous or a vicious type of human being, developed in an apparently random series of typical actions and speeches, and concluded with an explicit value judgment.

In a few of the resolves of the Short Century, Felltham makes use of aspects or techniques of the character genre. In S. 13, "A Christian's Valour and True Fidelity," one of the longest resolves in the 1623 collection, Felltham discusses two virtues of much importance to the Christian Stoic: "I obserue, besides the inward Contents of a peaceable conscience, two things, wherein a Christian excels all other men. In true Valour: In Fidelitie." In "a iust cause," the valiant Christian "is bold as a Lyon," for he knows that suffering is redemptive: there will be a reward in heaven. The wicked man sees death as a "shipwracke," but this valiant Christian sees it as "putting into harbour: where striking sayles, and casting Anchor, he returnes his lading with aduantage, to the owner; that is, his soule to God; leauing the bulke still mored in the Hauen; who is vnrigg'd, but onely to be new built again, and fitted for an eternall voyage."

The second half of this resolve concerns the Christians who are faithful to their God. They are described as the best friends any man can have: "This is that Fidelity that we finde, and admire in many, that haue chosen rather to embrace the flame, & dye in silence, then to reueale their Companions, and Brethren in Christ. Tyrants shal sooner want inuention for torments, Then they with tortures be made treacherous. The League that heauen hath made, hell wants power to breake. Who can separate the coniunction of the Deitie?"

This contemplation of faithful Christians is a series of statements, not pictures; and it does not very much resemble the character. However, when Felltham singles out one faithful Christian for further comment, the resultant description is akin to character writing: "Againe, as well in reproofe, as in kindnesse, doth his loue appeare. For howsoeuer hee conceales his friends faults, from the eye of the world; yet hee affectionately tels him of them, in priuate: not without some sorrow on his owne part, for his brothers fall. He scornes to be so base as to flatter: and he hates to bee so currish as to bite. In his reprehensions, he mingles Oyle and Vinegar: he is in them, plaine, and louing."

An element of the character obviously is present in this resolve: the sharp portrait of the faithful Christian friend is particularly characterlike. A clearly focused picture emerges from the apparently random list of typical actions that Felltham attributes to the faithful friend. Yet just as obviously, the elements drawn from character writing occupy little space in the resolve. In the whole of "A Christian's Valour and True Fidelity," Felltham's primary desire is not simply to present a portrait but to prove the thesis that, since a Christian is more valiant and faithful than other men, he is the most awful foe to an evil man and the very best friend to a good one. Felltham's resolves — even one such as S. 13, which is often cited as a character — stray very far from that genre.

What has impressed most critics of Owen Felltham's *Resolves*, from the seventeenth-century poet Thomas Randolph to the twentieth-century scholars George Williamson and McCrea Hazlett, is its style. In general, Felltham's contemporaries liked the style; eighteenth-century critics abhorred it; nineteenth-century commentators found it "quaint"; and twentieth-century critics are concerned with placing it in its proper relationship to the prose of Sir Francis Bacon and to the Circeronian-Senecan dispute of the earlier seventeenth century. Elizabethan Englishmen modeled their schoolboy compositions on the Latin of Cicero; and when they grew up and wrote their own books in English, they imitated the familiar Latin style. Ciceronian prose is oratorical and grand; its lengthy sentences are filled with subordinate clauses and rhetorical flourishes. Some English writers found the Ciceronian style appropriate, but others — especially toward the turn of the century — judged it unsuited to their purposes. Among this latter group, the neo-Stoics were leaders in the Ciceronian reaction, having found a classical style congenial to their philosophy in the terse, concise prose of Seneca. George Williamson, in a lengthy work on seventeenth-century English prose, characterizes the Senecan style as "pithy, short-breathed, grave, acute, and nervous."[11]

Joseph Hall, again an innovator, employed the Senecan style in his *Meditations and Vowes*; and Felltham followed suit in the resolves of 1623. Thomas Randolph's "To Mr. Feltham on his booke

of *Resolves*,"[12] a poem written sometime before 1628, is the earliest
known critical assessment of the work; and, as Williamson remarks,
"If we have any doubt of Felltham's Senecanism, Thomas Randolph
sets it at rest."[13] Randolph characterizes the "stile" of *Resolves* as
"pure and strong and round,/Not long but Pythy: being short
breath'd, but sound./ . . . . 'tis such/That in a little hath comprized
much. . . ." He finds such composition wholly appropriate to the
subject matter:

> Such is thy sentence, such thy stile, being read
> Men see them both together happ'ly wed.
> And so resolve to keepe them wed, as we
> Resolve to give them to posteritie.

To a generation reared primarily on Ciceronian fullness of rhetoric,
the style of the 1623 *Resolves* must have seemed remarkably terse
and pithy.

Felltham comments on the subject of style in two excogitations of
the Long Century (1628). In "Of the worship of Admiration" (L.
14), he praises Seneca's poetry for a quality he sought to imitate in
the prose of *Resolves*: "When I reade a rarely sententious man, I admire him, to my owne impatiency. I cannot reade some parts of
Seneca, aboue two Leaues together. He raises my soule to a contemplation, which sets me a thinking, on more, then I can imagine.
So I am forced to cast him by, and subside to an admiration." In "Of
Preaching" (L. 20), Felltham condemns lengthy sentences: "Long
and distended Clauses, are both tedious to the eare, and difficult for
their retaining. A Sentence well couch'd takes both the sense and the
vnderstanding. I loue not those Cart-rope speeches, that are longer
than the memorie of man can fathome. I see not, but that Diuinity,
put into apt significants, might rauish as well as Poetry."

In this passage Felltham is discussing prose designed to be heard
rather than read; but, significantly, he believes that good oratory
should approach the compactness and texture, the "apt significants," of poetry. Turning to the choice of words in an oration,
Felltham — much to the point of this discussion — quotes from one
of his favorite authorities: "this is *Seneca's* opinion: Fit words are
better than fine ones: I like not those that are in-iudiciously made;
but such as be expressiuely significant: that leade the minde to
something, beside the naked terme." Felltham prefers a combed
oration ("And kemb'd I wish it, not frizzled, nor curl'd") and "a

washed Language" in which all superfluities are rinsed away, leaving only judiciously chosen words that carry far-reaching intimations: "euen the *Scriptures*, (though I know not the *Hebrew*) yet I beleeue, they are penn'd in a tongue of deepe expression: wherein, almost euery word, hath a Metaphoricall sense, which does illustrate by some allusion."

Style, Felltham makes clear, should match the subject matter: "How politicall is *Moses*, in his *Pentateuch*? How philosophicall *Iob*? How massie and sententious is *Salomon* in his *Prouerbs*? how quaint, and flamingly amorous in the *Canticles*? how graue and solemne in his *Ecclesiastes*? that in the world there is not such an other dissection of the world as it. . . . How eloquent a pleader is *Paul* at the Barre? in disputation, how subtile." He applauds the Church Fathers, who wrote "with a crisped pen," but he warns that "I wish no man to bee too darke, and full of shaddow. There is a way to be pleasingly-plaine, and some haue found it."

This quality of plainness does not preclude all ornamentation, but it indicates that decoration which goes beyond good taste becomes gross rather than graceful: "I will honour [Divinity] in her plaine trimme: but I will wish to meet her in her graceful Iewels: not that they giue addition to her goodnesse: but that shee is more persuasiue in working on the soule it meetes with. When I meete with Worth which I cannot ouer loue, I can well endure that Art, which is a meanes to heighten liking." In summary, sentences should be short but pithy; words should be chosen with care to suggest something beyond their mere denotations; the style should fit the subject matter; and ornamentation — quotation, allusion, illustration — should be appropriate and tasteful. Such is a description of the Senecan style at its best, and such a style Owen Felltham strove to write in the 1620s.

Examples of the brief, pithy sentence are many in the 1623 resolves: "We haue seldome knowne him good, that refuseth to obey good order" (S. 81); "One bad voice, can put twenty good ones out of tune" (Ibid.); "The League that heauen hath made, hell wants power to breake" (S. 13). When sentences of the Short Century are lengthy, they normally are composed not by the piling up of subordinate clauses but by the adding of parallel ideas in coordinate constructions: "Enuie, like the worme, neuer runs but to the fairest and the ripest fruit: as a cunning Bloudhound, it singles out the fattest Deere of the Herd: 'tis a pitchy smoake, which wheresoeuer we finde, wee may be sure there is a fire of vertue" (S. 63); "A father is a

ready treasurie; a brother an infallible comfort; but a friend is both"
(S. 13).

The second aspect of good style, according to Felltham, lies in the
choice of words that suggest something beyond their primary
denotations. In "The great Good of Good Order" (S. 81), Felltham
speaks of the moon as having her "constant change," suggesting
both continual change and change within a constant pattern. In
"Content makes Rich" (S. 86), Felltham remarks that "to possesse
the whole world with a grumbling minde, is but a little more
specious pouerty." Here "specious" means "pleasant-seeming but
deceptive," but it also calls to mind "specie," from the same Latin
root, creating the powerful and effective oxymoron "monied poverty."

The third characteristic of good prose is fitness of style to subject
matter. One expects, for example, to find in "The Christians Life
what?" (S. 32) a nobler style than that in "A good Rule in wearing of
Apparell" (S. 58); and such is the case: "While blood is in our veines,
sinne is in our nature; since I cannot avoide it, I will learne to lament
it: and if through my offences, my ioy bee made obscure, and
vanish; that sorrow shall new beget my ioy; not because I haue
beene sinfull, but because, for sinne, I finde my selfe sorrowful" (S.
32); "Two things in my apparell, I will onely aime at; Com-
modiousnes, Decencie: beyond these I know not, how ought may be
commendable; yet I hate an effeminate sprucenesse, as much as a
phantasticke disorder. A neglectiue comlinesse is a man's best ornament" (S. 58). The range of style in the Short Century of *Resolves*
is rather limited, and justifiably so. Despite the large number of subjects discussed in the one hundred resolves, the book has only one
real subject, the attainment of the good life, of which the individual
topics are merely subordinate parts.

Another consideration of style involves ornamentation: the appropriateness of quotation, allusion, and illustration. Many of
Felltham's critics — especially in the nineteenth century — noted
the felicitous use of quotation and illustration in *Resolves*,[14] and two
examples show the correctness of their judgment. In the resolve "A
Rule for Spending and Sparing" (S. 29), Felltham warns: "Hee that
when hee should not, spends too much, shal when he would not,
haue too little to spend." To illustrate this aphoristic statement, he
draws on an incident reported by Diogenes Laertius (VI, 67):
" 'Twas a witty reason of *Diogenes*, why he asked a halfe-penny of
the thrifty man, and a pound of the prodigall; the first, hee said,

might giue him often, but the other e're long, would haue none to giue." On a more homely level, Felltham writes in "Three things aggrauate a Miserie" (S. 5): "Familiaritie takes away feare, when matters not vsuall, proue inductions to terror. The first time the Fox saw the Lyon, hee feared him as death: the second, hee feared him, but not so much: the third time hee grew more bold, and passed by him without quaking." Though known to every schoolboy, this illustration from Aesop nevertheless serves well to enforce the point that "Familiaritie takes away feare."

Compared to the prose of many other seventeenth-century writers and even to Felltham's later essays, the resolves of the Short Century contain relatively few quotations, allusions, and anecdotes. While several of the few ornamental devices that are present in these early resolves are commonplaces to the seventeenth century, cataloguing their sources is of value;[15] for the resulting list indicates quite clearly Felltham's intellectual and emotional bias toward Christian Stoicism. Felltham's favorite books of the Bible, as indicated by frequency of quotation and allusion, are Job and Ecclesiastes, both of special interest to the Stoically minded. Felltham also quotes Proverbs a few times, probably because of the aphoristic nature of the book; and he draws upon the Pentateuch and the Former Prophets frequently for illustration. Although he quotes or alludes to the Gospels, Epistles, and the Revelation rather sparingly, he does not totally neglect the New Testament. If frequency of allusion is any indication, Felltham's favorite pagan philosopher at the time of the Short Century was Diogenes the Cynic, a figure of much interest to the Stoic. So much is Diogenes a favorite that the young Felltham, evidently quoting from memory, often attributes to him remarks made by others.

The chief source of Felltham's knowledge of ancient philosophy was Diogenes Laertius whose *Lives of the Eminent Philosophers* he undoubtedly read in Latin translation. The moralist and biographer Plutarch he seems to have known rather well; he evidently had read the *Parallel Lives* in the 1603 edition of Sir Thomas North's English translation. That edition contains lives not present in the original Greek work, and Felltham alludes to these spurious lives more than once. He knew Homer in a Latin version; the fables of Aesop and La Fontaine; and a smattering of Virgil, Ovid, and Cicero. His direct knowledge of Seneca was at that time still slight; and he seems as yet to have read little by the Church Fathers, who were destined later to be some of his favorite sources for quotation and allusion.

Felltham's favorite kind of analogy, the illustrative metaphor, is striking enough to deserve special comment. In "Of Prayer" (S. 9), Felltham, considering his relatively unimportant position in the affairs of the world, draws a metaphor from chess: "while the game is playing, there is much difference between the King and the Pawne: that once ended, they are both shuffled into the bag together: and who can say whether was most happy, saue onely the King had many checks, while the little Pawne was free, and secure? My comfort is, my accesse to heauen is as free as the Princes. . . ." In one of the most characteristically Stoic of the resolves of the Short Century, Felltham contemplates "The vanitie and shortnesse of mans Life" (S. 57) in terms of a game of tennis: "he is in the Court of this world, as a ball bandyed between 2. rackets, Ioy & sorrow: If either of them strike him ouer, he may then rest: otherwise, his time is nothing, but a constant motion in calamitie." Passages such as these amply show Felltham's ability to write striking yet apt metaphors by employing a poetic kind of imagery that enriches the texture of both thought and statement.

A few of the Short Century resolves are so tightly controlled in metaphor and image that they might justifiably be termed prose exercises in the same kind of metaphysical wit found in much of the poetry of Felltham's day. Sir Herbert Grierson defines the metaphysical manner as "passionate, paradoxical argument, touched with humour and learned imagery."[16] "The vanitie and shortnesse of mans Life" (S. 57) and especially "A Christian compared in a three-fold condition to the Moone" (S. 28) have in them all the elements of Grierson's definition except possibly intentional humor.

In "The vanitie and shortnesse of mans Life," Felltham divides life into four parts, following Pythagoras: "He is first *Puer*, then *Iuuenis*, next *Vir* and after *Senex*" (boy, youth, young man, old man). The body of the piece catalogs in a meditation typical of Christian Stoic writers the problems encountered in each of these four periods. In the conclusion, which is not quite a resolve, the eighteen-year-old Owen Felltham comments that he has not yet passed the first of these stages and that he does not know whether he will be allowed the full measure of all four. If he is not, he states, he rests content that an early death is God's will. Nevertheless, "though I wish not the full fruition of all, yet doe I desire to borrow a letter from each: So instead of *Puer, Iuuenis, Vir, & Senex;* give mee the foure first letters, which will make me P I V S." The conclusion of a serious meditation with a clever acrostic on "pious" reveals that its author possessed a youthful delight in wit that cannot be held entirely in check by decorum; and the resolve suffers accordingly. Felltham leads himself into the same kind of trap that John Donne set for himself in punning on his own name in the serious religious poem "A Hymn to God the Father." Undoubtedly both Donne and Felltham were writing from conviction in these two works, but the results are so clever that the reader tends to question the sincerity behind the composition of the poem and the resolve.

A more complex use of metaphor, and one that can in all confidence be labeled metaphysical, controls "A Christian compared in a three-fold condition to the Moone" (S. 28) — a resolve as carefully constructed as a poem: "Wee see in the Moone a threefold condition, her Wane, her Increase, her Full: all which, I liuely see resembled in a Christian, three causes working them: Sinne, Repentance, Faith." Each of the correspondences is developed at some length: sin diminishes the Christian's glory, repentance increases it, and faith makes it shine in fullness. Felltham then draws a further comparison between the moon and the Christian: "for as the Moone when shee is least visible, is a Moone as well, as when wee see her in her full proportion; onely the Sunne lookes not on her vvith so full an aspect, and shee reflects no more, then she receiues from him: So a Christian in his lowest ebb of sorrow, is the Childe of God, as well, as when hee is in his greatest flow of comfort, onely the Sunne of Righteousnesse darts not the beames of his loue so plentifully, and he shews no more then God giues him."

After thus enriching the metaphor with the idea that the light of the moon is merely the reflected glory of the sun, Felltham concludes the resolve with the metamorphosis of the moon into the sun: "Sinne may cast me in a trance, it cannot slay me: it may bury my heat for a time, it cannot change my beeing: it may accuse, it shal not condemn: Though GOD depriue mee, pollish mee, and crowne mee for euer: where the Moone of my inconstant ioy shall change to a Sunne, and that Sunne shal neuer set, be clouded, or eclypsed." This resolve is one of the most tightly controlled pieces in the Short Century; and because of that control, the complete appropriateness of the metaphor, and the obvious sincerity that underlies the wit employed in it, Felltham reaches in it a high level of art.

The resolves of the Short Century are at once personal and impersonal. Some of the pieces do give the impression, despite the fact that they were published soon after their composition, of being written originally for Felltham's private use. As McCrea Hazlett describes them, they are "moral guides by which the author can right himself, if necessary."[17] This function cannot be denied, but its importance relative to other considerations can be questioned since Hazlett too easily concludes that "Felltham conceived his resolves to be as personal in their function as they are in their tone."[18]

The Christian humanist, and especially the Christian Stoic, tried to give the impression of artlessness while at the same time making effective use of a whole panoply of rhetorical devices. One of his most common ploys was the protest that he wrote only for himself; but, since he saw himself as an everyman, he concluded that what was helpful to him in striving toward the good life was of use to all. Noting mankind's resistance to exhortation, he sought to teach by example. While not questioning the sincerity of Felltham's assertion that these early resolves were aimed in "most respect to my selfe" ("To the Pervser"), they were — by extension — aimed at all seekers after wisdom and are consequently "personal" in a very restricted sense. The pronoun "I," occurring frequently in the resolutions which conclude the individual pieces, is the individualized Owen Felltham to be sure; but "I" is also the reader. The early resolves are, as Hazlett remarks, "nearly devoid of devices to persuade others."[19] The important word in this assessment is "devices," for the pieces avoid overt argumentation and are persuasive by quiet example.

These first one hundred resolves by Owen Felltham are not personal essays as that genre is now understood. The personal essay may include the author's past actions and observations, his past or present thoughts; but it does not admit resolutions for future behavior. Furthermore, the Owen Felltham of the 1623 *Resolves* is a somewhat undifferentiated man who reveals little of his individual peculiarities and nothing of the outward events of his life. Felltham emerges in the Short Century as a rather excessively pious, otherwise indistinct and slightly aloof personality. Some excesses of piety may be attributed to Felltham's youth at the time of the book's composition; like serious young men in all ages, he is proud of his piety and eager to share it. Douglas Bush's comment on the young Sir William Cornwallis, whose *Essays* appeared in 1600 - 1601, applies to the Owen Felltham of the Short Century of *Resolves*: "if it were not for references to his youth, we might think so sage a moralist, so disillusioned a critic of society, was a lean and slippered pantaloon."[20] The reader has to remind himself often that the 1623 *Resolves* were written by a youth "but Eighteen."

Some unattractive features of his persona are the result of genre. Felltham exhibits in 1623 only traces of the charity, good sense, and love of life and literature that he shows in the 1628 and 1661 essays — not necessarily because he did not yet possess those qualities but because the form of essay he chose, the resolve, does not lend itself to displaying those qualities. The *Resolves* of 1623 are formal exercises; they were written, for the most part, to conform to a rather rigid pattern. The seventeenth-century resolve allows for no such autobiographical anecdote or chatty informality as is frequently found in the personal essay. Moreover, the resolve by its very nature, is designed to aid man in his striving toward ultimate goodness; and anyone who writes only resolves runs the risk of giving the impression that he is always serious and always critical of the world around him.

The totally serious and overly pious qualities of the 1623 *Resolves* undergo a pleasing moderation, however, as Felltham proceeds from youth into young manhood — observing more, learning more, tolerating more. He discards as he goes the more formal and idealistic restrictions of the resolve, and he adopts a form broader in scope and more conducive to interesting elaborations and digressions: the excogitation of the Long Century.

III   *The Excogitations of the Long Century (1628)*

Additions made to *Resolves: Divine, Morall, Politicall* in 1628 are substantial. To the original one hundred short resolves, Felltham added a second, longer century, thereby quadrupling the size of the book. These additions represent an expansion of both subject matter and genre. Though he retained most of his earlier attitudes, the twenty-three-year-old Felltham included in the 1628 essays subjects more worldly than those considered in 1623; however, such titles as "Of Woman" (L. 30), "Of Dreames" (L. 52), "Of Logicke" (L. 55), "Of Poets and Poetrie" (L. 70), and others of a similar nature should not mislead one to believe the new essays are exclusively secular. Even when the subject might be considered profane, Felltham's treatment of it is such that the contemplation always includes a religious or ethical question: virtue in "Of Woman," the recognition of man's darker inclinations in "Of Dreames," faith versus reason in "Of Logicke," and the ennobling of the soul in "Of Poets and Poetrie."

These new pieces are labeled "excogitations," and the distinction is significant. Whereas the emphasis of the 1623 pieces is on the practical application to be drawn from meditation, the resolve itself, the new pieces added in 1628 have their emphasis on the "thinking out" section, the meditation proper; and the resolve element shrinks in importance or, in some cases, disappears altogether. The meditation as a genre, then, deserves attention;[21] and Bishop Joseph Hall again provides a useful starting point. In *The Arte of Divine Meditation* (1606), he defines, discusses, and gives examples of the forms of meditation as he understood them. A close examination of the excogitations in the Long Century of *Resolves* shows that Felltham either knew Hall's book or had reached a similar understanding of one of these forms through independent observation, for Felltham's pieces are closely related to "Extemporal" meditations.

Hall defines this particular kind of meditation as one "occasioned by outward occurrences offered to the mind,"[22] and he lists ten "forms of discourse" found in it:

1. We begin with some Description of that we meditate of.
2. Follows an easy and voluntary Division of the matter meditated.
3. A consideration of the Causes thereof, in all kinds of them.
4. The consideration of the Fruits and Effects.
5. Consideration of the Subject wherein, or whereabouts it is.
6. Consideration of the Appendances and Qualities of it.
7. Of that which is Diverse from it, or Contrary to it.
8. Of Comparisons and Similitudes, whereby it may be most fitly set forth.
9. The Titles and Names of the thing considered.
10. Consideration of fit Testimonies of Scripture, concerning our theme.

Hall notes that a meditation need not contain all ten parts and that the parts need not occur in the order listed. An examination of Hall's own meditations shows, moreover, that the "fit Testimonies" of the tenth part are often expanded to allow quotations from secular literature.

Most of the excogitations of the Long Century are extemporal meditations, and Felltham's "Of the Worship of Admiration" (L. 14), reproduced in several modern anthologies of seventeenth-century prose,[23] contains all ten elements of the genre as outlined by Hall. Admiration is described in terms of its effects: "Whatsoeuer is rare, and passionate, carries the soule to the thought of Eternitie. And, by contemplation, giues it some glympses of more absolute perfection, then here 'tis capable of." A division into parts is inherent in Felltham's description: admiration of worldly things (the "Royaltie of a State-show," a beautiful singing voice, or moral poetry) leads naturally to admiration of the ideal ("the worship of the Deity"). Felltham admits that he does not know what causes man to be so profoundly affected by admiration ("this I can but grope after. I can neither finde, nor say, what it is"), but he is certain where admiration resides (in the soul) and what its ultimate effect can be (a contemplation of the Deity generating right conduct in man). And upon reaching its highest expression, admiration acquires other names or titles (meditation, worship).

Several contrasts suggest themselves to Felltham in the course of this meditation: worthwhile poetry (Seneca's tragedies are the example used) leads to "grauity and seriousnesse," but "light aires turne vs into sprightfull actions; which breathe way in a loose laughter." Yet even the latter can be of benefit, since Felltham is mindful throughout the excogitation that man has both a spiritual and a corporal existence. "Mirth" can be "the excellency for the body" as "meditation" is "for the soule." Man's dual nature suggests yet another contrast, one in which the opposites complement each other: "I perswade no man to make [contemplations of the Deity] his whole life's businesse. Wee haue bodies, as well as soules. And euen this World, while we are in it, ought somewhat to be cared for." Relying on a common Renaissance idea that the human body is a microcosm of the world, Felltham argues that contemplation itself is not enough, that it should generate right action: "As those States are likely to flourish, where execution followes sound advisements: So is Man, when contemplation is seconded by action. Contemplation generates; Action propogates. Without the first, the latter is defectiue. Without the last, the first is but abortiue, and embrious."

The "Comparisons and Similitudes" of Hall's list are, in rhetorical terms, metaphors and similes. Only one metaphor in "Of the Worship of Admiration" is original with Felltham, but it is striking: "Meditation is the soules Perspective glasse: whereby, in her long remoue, shee discerneth God, as if hee were neerer hand." For the other metaphors and similes in the excogitation, Felltham relies on quotations from authorities(Hall's "fit Testimonies"): "Saint *Bernard* compares contemplation to *Rachel*, vvhich vvas the more faire: but action to *Leah*, vvhich vvas the more fruitfull"; and "He vvas a Monke of an honester age, that being asked hovv he could indure that life, vvithout the pleasure of bookes, ansvvered: The Nature of the Creatures vvas his Library: vvherin, vvhen hee pleased, he could muse vpon Gods deepe Oracles."

Quotations from authorities provide Felltham with more than

metaphor; they serve to strengthen his arguments and, of perhaps more importance, to suggest the continuity of human experience, thereby providing his own work with a sense of timelessness. A couplet from *Epistolarum ex Ponto* shows that even "the soft-soul'd *Ovid*" recognized "Sacred vigor" as the inspiration behind moral poetry. And a quotation from Plato reenforces Felltham's conclusion that man can achieve perfect happiness only by joining to his contemplation "a constant Imitation of God. In Justice, Wisdome, Holiness."

"On the Worship of Admiration" is — with the exception of the resolve element present in it — an extemporal meditation as described by Hall. The resolve is brief and relatively unobtrusive: "I vvill neither alvvayes be busie, and doing: nor euer shut vp in nothing but thoughts." The intrusion of the resolve is diluted even further by the fact that three sentences of a meditative nature follow it, denying it the concluding position in the work.

Even though "On the Worship of Admiration" and most of the other excogitations of the Long Century suggest that Felltham wrote with a formula in mind, the pieces nevertheless give the impression of spontaneity. The meditation genre allows much flexibility, for it admits more diverse subjects than does the resolve; it allows — even encourages — a wide range of rhetorical devices; and it permits much freedom in the selection and arrangement of its parts. The piece may even develop by suggestion rather than by strict rhetorical rules. One might not expect, for example, that a work whose announced subject is the "worship of admiration" will develop in such a way that its conclusion can satisfactorily be a resolution to mix contemplation with action. Yet nowhere in Felltham's excogitation on the subject is there a leap in logic or a sharp break in the progression of ideas. One idea suggests another, which in turn suggests a third, leading off in a somewhat unexpected yet perfectly satisfying direction. Such, of course, is the principle of development exploited by Montaigne in the creation of the personal essay; and the excogitations of 1628 show Felltham moving toward that French model. He is, nevertheless, somewhat restricted by formulae, by his hortatory purpose, and by his self-consciousness in the use of language.

One other question concerning genre arises: the influence of the character on the excogitations of the Long Century. The occasional pictures of human beings having virtues or vices present in such excogitations as "Of Pouertie" (L. 18), "Of Modestie" (L. 77), "Of

Detraction" (L. 50), "Of Ostentation" (L. 80), and especially "Of
Puritans" (L. 5) are reminiscent of the character; but these essays are
more than characters. Felltham allows himself much room to move
about within these pieces. He examines vices and virtues in themselves, rather than simply describing men who have them; he brings
in examples and illustrations from history and literature; and he
often juxtaposes in the same essay a vice or virtue and its opposite —
none of these things a character writer may do. As with the Short
Century resolves, the Long Century excogitations owe a little to the
character tradition; but none are true characters.

Just as the meditation allows more freedom of subject and
development than the resolve, the longer form also encourages
diversity in sentence structure. Owen Felltham did not lose his
fondness for aphoristic statement between 1623 and 1628, but the
pieces of the Long Century tend to be less dominated by aphorisms
than do the resolves of 1623. Simple, compound, and even complex
sentences — usually restricted to one subordinate clause each — sur-
round aphoristic statements and provide transition and explanation:
"As there bee many, that in their life assume too great a Libertie; so
I beleeve there are some, that abridge themselves of what they
might lawfully use. Ignorance is an ill Steward, to provide for either
soule, or Body. A man that submits to reverent Order, that
sometimes unbends himselfe in a moderate relaxation; and in all,
labours to approve himselfe, in the serenenesse of a healthful
Conscience: such a *Puritane* will I love immutably" (L. 5, "Of
Puritans"). The aphorism ("Ignorance is an ill Steward . . .") is so
well prepared for and its application is so well drawn out that it acquires a naturalness not always attendant upon the aphorisms of the
Short Century.

One notable aspect of the diction of the Long Century excogitations is the frequency of neologisms, words that nineteenth-
century critics often found fantastic and "barbarous."[24] Neologisms
are by no means completely absent from the 1623 or 1661 essays;
throughout his life, Felltham shows interest in creating new,
strikingly connotative words. This practice reached a zenith in 1628,
however. The newly coined words in the Long Century number well
over one hundred, and they are consequently an important aspect of
Felltham's style.

The neologisms that Felltham created are primarily of three
types.[25] One kind uses a noun or an adjective as a verb or a verbal:
"nor does the sedulous Bee, *thyme* all her thighes from one Flowres

single vertues" (L. 12, "That a wise man may gaine by any company"); "though pleasure *merries* the Sences for a while: yet horror
after *vultures* the vnconsuming heart . . ." (L. 25, "Of the horror
sinne leaues behind"). A second kind employs affixes: "The Papists
pourtray [God] as an old Man: and by this meanes, *disdeifie*
him . . ." (L. 16, "Of the choice of Religion"); "Even blushing
brings [maidens] to their *Devirgination* . . ." (L. 77, "Of Modestie"). "Inkhorn terms," derived primarily from Latin, are the third
type: "how like a *nated* Sop . . ." (L. 12, "That a wise man may
gaine by any company"); "nor is ther any whom Calamity doth so
much *tristitiate*, as that he neuer sees the flashes of some warming
ioy" (L. 41, "That all things are restrained").

Felltham creates in many of his neologisms a "Metaphoricall
sense, which does illustrate by some allusion" (L. 20, "Of
Preaching"). The suggestion of aroma in the verb "to thyme," the
powerful allusion to Prometheus' torture in "to vulture," and the
myriad associations of "to merry" contribute immeasurably to the
texture of the sentences in which these words appear. "To disdeify,"
besides being pleasantly alliterative, is the most economical and
striking way possible to indicate the removing of all majesty from the
idea of God; and, at the opposite pole, there is a playful cleverness in
"devirgination." Perhaps the Latinate words are, as a whole, the
least effective of Felltham's neologisms. Most are, like "nated"
(born, bred, framed by nature), not particularly necessary since good
words with the same meaning exist in the language. Occasionally,
however, neologisms derived from Latin are powerful and sugges-
tive, as is "tristitiate" (make sorrowful).

Felltham also uses commonly accepted words in striking, connotative ways. The style of The Song of Solomon is "flamingly
amorous" (L. 20, "Of Preaching"); music is "wanton'd Ayre" (L. 88,
"Of Musicke"); and mirth is a "Pattent" which adds "time and happines to the crazed life of Man"(L. 5, "Of Puritans"). The worlds of
politics and commerce enrich thought about the world of the spirit in
"Of Idlenesse" (L. 48): "How bright does the Soule grow with use
and negotiation!" That every sublunary thing dies is stated in terms
of gluttony: "With what a generall swallow, Death still gapes vpon
the generall world" (L. 47, "Of Death"). To indicate that the uni-
form — and what it represents — is more important than the man
wearing it, Felltham employs a strikingly connotative verbal: "How
vnseemly is it, when a graue Cassocke shall be lin'd with a wanton
Reueller, and with crimes, that make a loose one odious" (L. 91, "Of

Scandall"). And a well-chosen homonym in "Of Charitie" (L. 86) adds allusive power: "Charitie is communicated goodnesse, and without this, Man is no other then a Beast, preying for himselfe alone." The most beautiful language in the Long Century occurs in "Of the Soule" (L. 64). Suggesting both vegetative growth and the description of a comet, Felltham calls the human soul "a shoot of everlastingnesse." So poetic is the metaphor that Henry Vaughan appropriated it for use in "The Retreate."

Since the subject matter in the Long Century is much broader than that in the Short Century, a wider range of styles is possible. At one extreme is solemnity: "There is no Spectacle more profitable, or more terrible, then the sight of a dying man, when hee lyes expiring his soule on his death-bed: to see how the ancient society of the body and the soule is divelled [rent asunder]; and yet to see, how they struggle at the parting: being in some doubt what shall become of them after" (L. 47, "Of Death"). At the other, playfulness: "They which talke too much to others, I feare me, seldome speake with themselues enough: and then, for want of acquaintance with their owne bosomes, they may well bee mistaken, and present a Foole to the People, while they thinke themselues are wise. But there are, and that severally, that be much troubled with the disease of speaking. For, assuredly, Loquacity is the Fistula of the minde; ever running, and almost incurable" (L. 93, "Of tediousnesse in Discourse").

Since the excogitation, modeled as it is on the meditation, allows — and, indeed, demands — ornamentation, the Long Century essays, not surprisingly, are filled with more quotation, allusion, and analogy than can be found in the Short Century resolves. In 1628, Felltham's favorite books of the Bible continue to be Ecclesiastes and Job; and Diogenes the Cynic remains his favorite among ancient Greek philosophers. Felltham knows more of Seneca than he did in 1623, and he quotes frequently from that philosopher's letters and tragedies. He does not seem much conversant with Marcus Aurelius, whose work was not widely read until the eighteenth century; but he does appear to know Epictetus. Of obvious appeal is Boethius, and Felltham quotes several of the metra from *The Consolation of Philosophy*. He has read more Ovid, and his favorite works are *Tristia* and the verse letters from Pontus that were written during the Roman poet's period of exile and are filled with dark musings on fate, injustice, and inhumanity.

Of the other Latin poets, the satirists Horace and Juvenal are quoted at length, as are Martial and Ausonius, whose epigrams dot the pages of the excogitations. Felltham also finds a place for the comedies of Plautus and Terence. Plutarch remains his favorite among ancient biographers; but he also has read Suetonius, Lucan, and Livy, as well as scattered bits of Dion Cassius, Ammianus, Florus, and Nepos. Of the other Classical writers, he frequently quotes Cicero; rather surprisingly, he includes a bit of the *Satyricon* of Petronius Arbiter; and he alludes to Pliny's and Aristotle's works about natural history. He relies heavily on the writings of such Church Fathers as Augustine, Jerome, Bernard, Gregory, and Chrysostum. Of Felltham's near contemporaries, only two besides Bishop Hall appear influential: Lipsius, the great neo-Stoic philosopher of the sixteenth century; and Montaigne, whose work Felltham probably read in Florio's English translation since he did not yet know French.

The essays of the Long Century employ many worldly illustrations drawn from the same fields as those in the Short Century: sailing and gentlemanly sport; but to these are added metaphors based on music and war. Drawing attention to the knowledge that a skillful mariner must have, Felltham argues that virtue thrives only when it is un-cloistered: "Those that are throughly arted in Nauigation, doe as well know the Coasts, as the Ocean; as well the Flawes, the Sands, the Shallowes, and the Rockes; as the secure depths, in the most vnperillous Channell. So, I think, those that are perfect men, (I speake of perfection since the fall) must as well know bad, that they may abtrude it; as the good, that they may embrace" (L. 12, "That a wise man may gaine by any company"). In another essay, Felltham turns to fencing for illustration of the same point: "He that is to play with a cunning Fencer, will heed his Wardes, and advantage more; who, were he to meet with one vnskilfull, hee would neglect, or not thinke of them. Strong opposition teaches opposition to be so" (L. 28, "Of being overvalued").

Fishing provides Felltham with two striking aphorisms. In "Of Preaching" (L. 20), he writes of the power that a good public speaker can exert: "Diuinitie well ordered, casts forth a Baite, which angles the Soule into the eare: and how can that cloze; when such a guest sits in it?" The metaphor may be mixed; it is, nonetheless, effective. The other metaphor based on fishing is unmixed, and it shows that Felltham obviously knew something of that recreation first hand. In "Against Compulsion" (L. 51), he writes: "Little Fishes are twitched vp with the violence of a sudden pull; when the like action cracks the line, whereon a great one hangs."

Two good illustrations are drawn from hunting: "Publike

Reproofe, is like striking of a Deere in the Herd; it not onely wounds him, to the losse of inabling blood: but betrayes him to the Hound, his Enemie: and makes him, by his fellowes, be pusht out of companie" (L. 8, "Of Reprehension") and ". . . Fame often playes the Curre, and opens, when shee springs no game" (L. 23, "That no man can be good to all").

Felltham liked music when he felt that it moved men to virtue and not to vice ("Of Musicke," L. 88), and he drew on the art to illustrate order and degree: "As in Musicke sometimes one string is lowder, sometimes another; yet neuer one long, nor neuer all at once: So sometimes one State gets a Monarchy, sometimes another; sometimes one Element is violent, now another; yet neuer was the whole world vnder one long, nor were all the Elements raging together. Every string has his vse, and his tune, and his turne" (L. 41, "That all things are restrained").

Felltham probably had not seen war firsthand when he wrote the resolves of the Long Century. Nevertheless, he occasionally uses war instruments as metaphors. In a Stoic mood, he asks: "is content such a slender tittle, that 'tis nothing but the present now; fled sooner than enioy'd? like the report of a lowd-tongu'd Gunne, ceas'd as soone as heard: without any thing to shew it has been, saue remembrance only" (L. 22, "Of our sense of absent Good").

Some of Felltham's better metaphors are topical allusions that, unless annotated, are often lost on the modern reader: "Thy vices an enemy sets, like *Pauls*, on high; for the gaze of the world, and the scatter'd Citie: Thy Vertues, like Saint *Faiths*, hee placeth vnder ground, that none may note them" (L. 21, "Of reconciling Enemies"). Anyone who has seen C. J. Vischer's panorama of London (1616) knows how completely St. Paul's Cathedral dominates the city's skyline; it takes a little effort to discover that St. Faith's was a church in the crypt of St. Paul's and was completely hidden from view. With this information supplied, however, the strength of the metaphor asserts itself.

While the excogitations of 1628 show a young man more tolerant, more interesting, and more likeable than the youth of the 1623 resolves, the picture of Felltham that emerges from this second set of essays is not entirely without flaw. Occasionally he feels compelled to prove himself. In "To the Readers," he drops the overly modest attitude adopted in 1623; he professes himself to be a gentleman and explains his reasons for having written and published the new essays: "If you aske why I writ them; 'twas because I lou'd my Study. If, why I publish them, know, that hauing no other meanes to shew my selfe to the World, so well, I chose this; not to boast, but because I would not deceiue." Worthy reasons, certainly; but there is the nagging suggestion that the emphasis is on showing himself to the world rather than on avoiding deception. Furthermore, one finds in the 1628 *Resolves* the hint that Felltham is not completely natural, that he may be writing what he believes the world wishes to hear.

Also, some of the Long Century excogitations betray the naiveté of a young man who has not seen much of the world or its affairs. His essay "Of Warre, and Souldiers" (L. 90) is a good example of naive theories wrought in a bookish atmosphere. He compares war to medicine: "After a long Scene of Peace, Warre ever enters the Stage; and indeed, is so much of the worlds Phisicke, as it is both a Purge, and blood-letting." And he draws a rather startling conclusion concerning the invention of gunpowder: "For the weapons of War, they differ much from those of ancient times: and I beleeue, the invention of Ordnance hath mightily saved the liues of men. They command at such distance, and are so vnresistable, that men come not to the shock of a Battell, as in former Ages. We may obserue, that the greatest numbers, haue falne by those weapons, that haue brought the Enemies neerest together."

The essays of the Revised Short Century, written after Felltham had lived through the Civil War, contain nothing but the most damning references to war; and they praise its opposite in a moving contemplation ("Of Peace," R.S. 84). In the few instances when the excogitations of the Long Century disappoint, they do so because of their author's youth and lack of experience. The years between 1628 and 1661 mellowed Owen Felltham; and he is at his warmest, wisest, most natural, and best in the essays of the Revised Short Century.

IV   *The Personal Essays of the Revised Short Century (1661)*

In the 1661 edition of *Resolves*, the one hundred brief pieces of 1623 are missing, having been replaced by a "century" of eighty-five lengthy essays. Of these, sixty-two are revisions of resolves in the original group, and twenty-three are wholly new works.[26] So lengthy are they that in this edition of Felltham's book — the first in folio — eighty-five of them cover 204 pages, while the one hundred excogitations of 1628 occupy only 172. In the preface of this 1661 edition, "To the Reader," the printer (or more likely Felltham himself, writing in the third person) comments on this substitution:

The Reader may please to be informed, That the latter part of these Resolves, formerly Printed as the first Century; the Author, upon their perusal, could not himself be satisfied with them. For, however all seem'd to pass currant, and did arise to several Impressions; yet, being written when he was but Eighteen, they appear'd to him, to have too many young weaknesses, to be still continued to the World: though not for the Honesty; yet, in the Composure of them. . . . And that hath made him, in this Impression, to give them a new Frame, and various Composition; by altering many, leaving out some, and adding of others new. That now, upon the matter, they quite are other things.

The reason for the revision, then, is "the Composure," a term which includes the interrelated elements of genre, style, and tone. Just as the addition of the Long Century in 1628 represents a movement from the restrictive and relatively unornamented resolve to the more expansive and adorned excogitation, the substitution of the Revised Short Century in 1661 represents another shift in form and expression — one more subtle, but just as significant.

Felltham obviously was not sufficiently displeased with the composition of the excogitations of 1628 to revise or discard them in the 1661 edition of *Resolves*; they are reprinted there exactly in the form in which they had first appeared thirty-three years earlier. He evidently considered them to have no substantial "young weaknesses"; and in revising the Short Century resolves into the essays of 1661, he incorporated many characteristics of the 1628 meditation. Yet the 1661 essays differ not only from the 1623 resolves from which many of them sprung, but also from the 1628 excogitations which they superficially resemble. While the resolve element shrinks in importance in the 1628 pieces, it disappears almost altogether in the 1661 essays. Just as the excogitations are more expansive than the resolves, so the new essays are even more lengthy and diffuse. Though retaining his fondness for ornamenting his pieces with illustrations and examples drawn from Scripture, literature, and history, Felltham in 1661 relies more on personal experience and on independent judgment than he did previously. Still able to turn an aphorism, he writes the new essays in a phrasing more nearly conversational than that of the 1628 excogitations. Perhaps the most significant change of all is that while still a pious Christian, he is able in his mature years to rid himself of the last traces of affectation and stiffness. What Felltham terms the Second Century in the 1661 edition of his life's work are not "resolves," as the pieces are labeled, nor meditations, which they superficially resemble; they are personal essays.

As Douglas Bush remarks, "The Essay was born when Montaigne retired to his tower to take stock of himself and thereby of all human

experience."[27] The essays of Michel de Montaigne are relatively
brief prose works which are tentative in approach, free in form and
in the choice of subject matter, personal in illustration and application, and conversational in style. Montaigne was an early participant
in the reaction against Ciceronian style, and this bias not only explains his predilection for conversational prose but also helps to account for the essay form which he developed. Morris Croll has noted
that the purpose of the anti-Ciceronians "was to portray, not a
thought, but a mind thinking."[28] Other brief prose works of the
late Renaissance — notably the meditation, the vow, and the
resolve — frequently share with the essay this anti-Ciceronian im-
pulse, but may be distinguished from the essay in that they portray a
mind thinking toward a goal (the concluding vow or resolution
designed to better life and conduct) while the early essay shows a
mind thinking on a subject, with no formulaic conclusion in view.
The essay is wholly reflective, musing on the past and the present;
the meditation, the resolve, and the vow are anticipatory, making
moral plans for the future.

Sir Francis Bacon was the first Englishman to write short prose
pieces labeled "essays" (*Essayes*, 1597, revised and enlarged in 1612
and again in 1625); and his remain the best known early examples,
despite their atypical formality and aloofness. More nearly in the
Montaigne tradition are the essays of Sir William Cornwallis (1600 -
1601). Many collections of pieces called essays followed, including
those of Daniel Tuvill (1608, 1609), Thomas Tuke (1614), John
Stephens (1615, 1627), Geffray Mynshull (1618), Richard Braithwait
(1620), William Mason (1621), and John Robinson (1628).[29] There
are even essays discoverable in Ben Jonson's *Timber* (1640 - 1641).[30]
Some of the best seventeenth-century English essays, however, are
to be found in the Revised Short Century of Owen Felltham's
Resolves.

Many of the 1661 essays are made from 1623 resolves. The
changes made to turn the 1623 resolve "A Rule in reading Authors"
(S. 27) into the 1661 personal essay "Of reading Authors" (R. S. 27)
are typical of Felltham's method of revision. The most effective way
to indicate the nature and extent of those changes is to set the two
versions side by side:

"A Rule in reading Authors" (S. 27), 1623	"Of reading Authors" (R. S. 27), 1661
Some men read Authors as our Gentlemen vse flowers, onely for	The Comparison was very apt in the excellent *Plutarch*, That we ought

delight and smell; to please their
fancy, and refine their tongue.
Others like the Bee, extract onely
the hony, the wholesome precepts,
and this alone they beare away, leauing
the rest, as little worth, of small value.

to regard books as we would do
sweet-meats; not wholly to aim at
the pleasantest, but chiefly to
respect the wholesomeness:

not forbidding
either, but approving the latter most.
But to speak cleerly, though the
profitablenesse may be much more in
some Authors then there is in others,
yet 'tis very rare that the Ingenious
can be ill. He that hath wit to
make his pen pleasant, will have
much adoe to separate it from being
something profitable. A totall
Levity will not take. A Rich Suit
requires good stuffe, as well as to
be tinseld out with Lace and Ribbands.
And certainly, Wit is very neer a
kinne to wisdome. If it be to take in
generall, or to last; we may find, it
ought to be enterwoven with some
beautiful flowers of Rhetorique; with
the grateful scenting herbs of Reason,
and Philosophy, as well as with the
Simples of Science, or physical plants
and the ever green sentences of piety
and profoundnesse. Even the looser
Poets have some divine praeceptions.
Though I cannot but think *Martials*
wit was much cleaner then his pen,
yet he is sometimes grave as well as
Gamesome. And I do not find but
deep and solid matter, where 'tis
understood, takes better then the
light flashes and the skipking Capers
of Fancy. Who is it will not be as
much delighted with the weighty and
substantial lines of the *Seneca's*, and
Plutarch, the crisped *Salust*, the
politick *Tacitus*, and the well-breath'd
Cicero, as with the frisks and dancings
of the jocund and the airy Poets.
Those abilities that Renowned Authors
furnish the world with, beget a kind

of Deifical Reverence in their future
Readers. Though even in the unpartial-
ness of War, *Alphonsus* wanted stones
to carry on his Siege of *Cajeta*, and
none could be so conveniently had, as
from *Tullies Villa Formiana* that was
near it; yet for the noble regard he
bore to his long pass'd Eloquence, he
commanded his Souldiers that they
should not stir them. Composures
that aim at wit alone, like the Foun-
tains and Water-works in Gardens,
are but of use for recreation, after the
travails and toyls of more serious
imployments and studies. The Palace
and the constant dwelling is composed
of solid and more durable Marbles,
that represent to after-Ages the
Ingenuity and Magnificence of the
Architect. And as the House alone is
no compleat habitation, without these
decorations for delight; no more is
the work of the brain on all sides fur-
nished without some sprightly conceits
that may be intermixt to please.

Nec placeat facies cui Gelasinus abest.
   No Beauty has that face,
   Which wants a natural grace.

Those Romances are the best, that,
besides the contexture for taking the
Fancy in their various accidents,
gives us the best Idea's of Morality,
with the expressive Emanations of
wisdom, and divine knowledge. Those
that are light, and have only the
Gauderies of Wit, are but for youth
and greener years to toy withal.
When we grow to riper age, we begin
to leave such studies as sports and
pastimes, that we out-grow by more
maturity. Of this Age *Horace* was,
when he declar'd

   Nunc itaque & versus, & coetera
   ludicra pono:

*Quid verum, atque decens, curo
  & rogo, & omnis in hoc sum:
Condo, & compono, quae mox
  depromere possum.*

Now Rimes, and childish Fancies,
  quite are gone:
The graceful Truth I search; that
  rest upon,
And well digested, gravely put
  it on.

Jocular strains, they are but Spring-flowers; which though they please the eye, they yield but slender nourishment: They are the Autumn fruits, that we must thrive and live by; the Sage sayings, the rare Examples, the Noble Enterprises, the handsome Contrivances, the success of good and bad actions, the Elevations of the Deity, the motives and incitements to Vertue, and the like; are those that must build us up to the Gallantry and Perfection of Man. I do not find, but it may well become a man to pursue both the one, and the other, to precept himself into the practise of Vertue; and to fashion both his Tongue and Pen, into the exercise of handsome and significant words. He that foundations not himself with the Arts, will hardly be fit to go out Doctor either to himself, or others.

In reading I will care
for both; though for the last, most: the
one serues to instruct the mind; the other
fits her to tell what she hath learned:
pity it is, they should be deuided:

In reading I will be careful for both, though not equally. The one serves to instuct the mind, the other enables her to tell what she hath learn'd; the one without the other, is lame. What benefit yields fire, if still rak'd up in ashes; though flint may bear a flame in't: yet, we prize it but a little, because we cannot get it forth without knocking? He that hath worth in him, and cannot express it, is a chest of wood perhaps containing a Jewel, but who shall be better for't, when the key is lost.

he that hath
worth in him, and cannot expresse it
is a chest keeping a rich Iewell, and
the key lost. Concealing goodnesse, is
vice; vertue is better by being communi-

cated. A good stile, with wholesome
matter, is a faire woman with a vertuous soule, which attracts the eyes of
all; The good man thinkes chastly, and
loues her beauty, for her vertue; which
hee still thinks more faire, for
dwelling in so faire an outside. The
vicious man hath lustfull thoughts;
and he would for her beauty, faine
destroy her vertue; but coming to
sollicite his purpose, findes such
diuine lectures from her Angels
tongue, and those deliuer'd with so
sweet a pleasing modesty, that he
thinks vertue is dissecting her soule
to him, to rauish man with a beauty
which he dream'd not of. So hee
could not curse himselfe, for
desiring that lewdly, which he hath
learn'd since, onely to admire, and
reuerence: Thus he goes away better,
that came with an intent to bee worse.

                 Quaint
phrases on good subiect, are baits
to make an ill man virtuous:

A good style does sometimes take him,
that good matter would beat away:
'Tis the guilding, that makes the wholesome Pill be swallowed. Elegance
either in Tongue, or Pen, shews a man
hath minded something besides sports
and vice. 'Tis graceful to speak, or
to write proper; nor is it easie to
separate *Eloquence* and *Sapience*; for
the first leads to the other, and is
at least, the Anticourt to the Palace
of Wisdom. A good style, with good
matter, consecrates a work to Memory;
and sometimes while a man seeks
but one, he is caught to be a servant
to the other.

      how many vile men seeking these
haue found themselues Conuertites?

      I may refine my speech without
harme: but I will endeuour more to
reform my life. 'Tis a good grace both
of Oratory, or the Pen, to speake, or
write proper:

1623   1661

| | The Principal end of reading, is to inrich the mind. |

                             The Principal
end of reading, is to inrich the mind.
the next, to improve the Pen and Tongue.
'Tis much more gentile and sutable,
when they shall appear all of a piece.
but that is the best work, where   Doubtless, that is the best work,
the Graces and the Muses meet.   where the Graces and the Muses meet.

The original resolve and the subsequent personal essay are Felltham's musings on a common Renaissance critical principle that is stated, among other places, in Sir Philip Sidney's *The Defence of Poesie* (written about 1583; published, 1595). In his discussion of "heroical," or epic, poetry, Sidney refers to the Classical idea that a man "who could see vertue, would bee woonderfullie ravished with the love of her bewtie." The achievement of the epic poet lies in making virtue "more lovely in her holliday apparrell, to the eye of anie that will daine, not to disdaine untill they understand."[31] A poet's purpose in striving for beauty in his work is, then, to clothe his moral lesson in a pleasant form so that many will wish to read it and will, perhaps unknowingly, absorb the moral as they delight in the beauty that frames it.

The two ways that Felltham chose to express this Renaissance critical theory differ greatly. The first and most important difference is that the resolve element present in the 1623 version ("I may refine my speech without harme: but I will endeuour more to reforme my life.") is missing in the 1661 text. The only thing even approaching a resolve in the revised version occurs in a passage concerning wit and wholesome subject matter: "In reading I will be careful for both, though not equally." But this sentence is taken over, with no change in meaning, from the earlier version; and, significantly, this resolve-like statement seems out of place in its new surroundings. Throughout all the rest of this 1661 essay, Felltham is discussing what he has discovered through reading and experience; he is not preparing himself through meditation to make a resolution. Consequently, "In reading I will be careful for both" is an abrupt shift in point of view and in purpose. Though it is stated in personal terms, it is, ironically, an intrusion antithetical to the tone of the personal essay since it is anticipatory rather than reflective.

The second and most obvious difference between these two texts is length. Although the original resolve is a comparatively long one for its genre and although part of it is discarded in the revision, the resultant essay is almost three times its size. The frequent use of quotation and allusion accounts for much of the expansion. Although the 1623 resolve "A Rule in reading Authors" concerns literature, no quotation appears in it, and no author's name is mentioned. In the 1661 essay "Of reading Authors," Felltham paraphrases a passage from Plutarch, quotes Martial (VI, 25, 6) and Horace (*Epistolae* I, 1, 10 - 12), and mentions by name four other writers: Seneca, Sallust, Tacitus, and Cicero. The 1661 version also contains an illustration from history, the anecdote concerning Alfonso I of Este, Duke of Ferrara (1476 - 1534), who commanded the papal troops in the War of the League of Cambria (1509) and who three years later fought against Pope Julius II at Ravenna. Many such historical allusions appear in the Revised Short Century; almost none occur in the Short Century.

The expansion of aphorisms into statements that approach conversation is a key to the stylistic revisions made in turning the resolves of 1623 into the essays of 1661. In S. 27, the clause "In reading I will care for both" is followed by "though for the last, most," an elliptical clause which betrays the young author's fondness for terse, parallel statement. In R. S. 27, the corresponding clause "In reading I will be careful for both" is followed by "though not equally," a much more natural phrasing. In this second version, Felltham reserves for the sentences that follow the burden of indicating which of the two, virtue or wit, he thinks more important. Further along in both versions is another example of expansion. In 1623, the man who has "worth in him, and cannot express it, is a chest keeping a rich Iewell, and the key lost." In 1661, that same man is "a chest of wood perhaps containing a Jewel, but who shall be better for't, when the key is lost." The later version is a more cautious statement, and the question that is added, "who shall be better for't," shows Felltham's concern that his point not be missed.

The most revealing example of the shift from aphoristic to conversational style occurs near the end of both versions where Felltham states most explicitly the idea found in Sidney's *Apology*. The 1623 passage is an aphorism to which is added a question: "Quaint phrases on a good subject, are baits to make an ill man vertuous: how many vile men seeking these, haue found themselues Conuertites?" In 1661, Felltham treats this same idea in a more relaxed and informal manner: "A good style does sometimes take him, that good matter would beat away: 'Tis the guilding, that makes the wholesome Pill be swallowed. . . . and sometimes while a man seeks but one, he is caught to be a servant to the other." Not only is the pace more leisurely in the 1661 version, but the meaning — through expansion — is made plainer. Felltham is clearly writing, not for himself alone or for a small coterie of admirers, but for the "middle sort of people" spoken of in the preface to this 1661 edition of *Resolves*. He is writing to inform and to instruct the ordinary educated man, and such is one of the functions of personal essays.

A fourth difference between the resolves of his youth and the essays of his maturity concerns what Felltham discarded as he revised the early pieces, most notably in this instance the passage built around the "faire woman with a vertuous soul." It seems likely that the young Felltham pounced on the word "rauished" in Sidney's paraphrase of Plato and Cicero and that he built from it a lengthy illustration for his resolve. The mature Felltham, undoubtedly wishing to make his work appear less derivative, deleted this abstract and artificial illustration as he turned the resolve into the essay. Also discarded in the 1661 revision was the derivative opening statement of the 1623 resolve: "Some men read Authors as our Gentlemen vse flowers, onely for delight and smell. . . . Others like the Bee, extract onely the hony. . . ." This aphoristic passage is quite reminiscent of the Some/Other formula used frequently by Joseph Hall and other Senecans, as in Francis Bacon's 1597 essay "Of Studies": "Some books are to bee tasted, others to be swallowed, and some few to be chewed and digested. . . ." In cutting out these passages, Felltham in great measure ceases to be dependent on bookish models and moves toward a more confident reliance on his own experience and judgment. For instance, in R. S. 27 he not only refers specifically to several authors, which he had not done in the 1623 resolve, but he also gives us his opinion of them. Martial is witty, but not particularly "clean"; Seneca and Plutarch are "weighty and substantial"; Tacitus is "politick"; and Cicero is "well-breath'd." But, while Felltham comes to a greater reliance on his own judgment, he by no means excludes metaphor, allusion, and quotation from the personal essays of 1661. Indeed, such ornaments are more appropriate to this form than to the resolve or the excogitation. The difference in genre effects, however, a difference in the way these devices are used.

The changes that Felltham made in turning the resolve of 1623 into the personal essay of 1661 remove both affectation and stiffness by discarding the resolve formula, expanding the text in both length and scope, turning the aphoristic statement into the conversational, and relying on personal experience and independent judgment. The resultant essay is more natural in statement and tone than the formal resolve or even the meditation could ever be.

Although Felltham's personal experiences and judgments color much of R. S. 27, the twenty-three essays newly written for the 1661 collection show more clearly the author's personality asserting itself. There events in Felltham's life inform and enrich comments on such topics as memory (R. S. 17), superstition (R. S. 36), history (R. S. 38), gambling (R. S. 58), business (R. S. 67), dancing (R. S. 70), almsgiving (R. S. 79), law (R. S. 82), conscience (R. S. 83), and Divine Providence (R. S. 85). "Of Peace" (R. S. 84), a new composition, is especially noteworthy for its reliance on personal observation and for its reflection of Felltham's maturity and wisdom. The essay begins with a reference to the ancient idea of Divine Order: "If men knew rightly, how to value Peace; as is the Empyreal Heaven, this lower world might be. Where all the motions of the comprehending Orbs, all the several Constellations, and the various Position of the Stars, and Planets, produce a beauteous Chorus, and a Harmony truly ravishing."

In the 1628 meditation "Of Warre, and Souldiers," Felltham justified war by comparing the body politic to the human body; in the 1661 essay "Of Peace," that same analogy extolls the benefits of peace:

As health to the body, so peace is to the soul. What is wealth, or wit, or honour, when want of health shall ravish from us all pleasure in them? And what are all the enrichings, the embellishings, and the Imbrockadoings of Fortune to us, when War shall tear these off and trample on our Glories? The richest Wines, the choisest Viands, by sickness prove insipid. The silk does lose his softness, the silver his bright hue, and the gold his pleasing yellow. As the sense of feeling is the ground of all the rest, and active life does cease when that is lost: So is health the foundation of felicities, and the want of its joys privation: yet is it Peace that gives them tast and rellish, and affords the sweet enjoyment of all that can be procured.

Turning to Biblical authority in the second paragraph,[32] Felltham paraphrases Philippians 4:7 and quotes directly Luke 2:14: "Though the other Attributes of God are no doubt beyond our comprehension, yet, this more emphatically is said to pass all our understanding. Next his own Glory, 'twas the establishing this, invited God from Heaven. The first branch of that Celestial Proclamation, was, *Glory be to God on high*; the next was, *On Earth Peace*." Elaborating still further on the attributes of peace, Felltham says that it "is the cement between the Soul and Deity, between Earth and Heaven. It leads us softly up the milky way, and ushers us with Musick to the Presence of Divinity, where all her Rarities are heap'd and strew'd about us. The enjoyment of Friends, the improvement of Arts, the sweetness of Natures delicacies, the fragrancy of Fruits and Flowers, the flourishing of Nations, and those pleasing contentions, that stream out themselves from all Heroick Vertues are all brought in, and glorified by Peace.''

In considering the effects of war on the weak and the strong, Felltham concludes that it harms both: "Peace helps the weak and indigent; and health and soundness too, to the sick endeavours. . . . But, War kills men in health, preys only on the soundest; and, like the savage Lyon, does seize the valiant soonest, as thinking the old and impotent too mean to be his quarry.'' Then, with Hannibal as an illustration, Felltham points out that only too frequently a victory in war is a Pyrrhic one; and, with Alexander and Caesar as examples, he shows that victory often leads to a pride and an insolence in the conqueror that create yet more wars: "Success does flame the bloud to pride and boldned insolence; and as often kindles new as it does conclude old Wars. One world sufficed not *Alexander*. Nor could all the *Roman* Territories set bound to *Caesars* limitless ambition. For, when we once put off from the shore of Peace, we lanch into the Sea that's bottomless. We swim on angry waves, and are carryed, then as the wind of Fortune drives us.''

The most striking illustration in the essay is not derived from biblical materials, literature, or ancient history, but from events in England that Felltham himself had lived through. He uses England's woes during the Civil Wars as a microcosm in which to view the condition of the whole world in all times:

If any man will see in little (for what is an Island or two, to the world?) Let him but well consider, the havock that a few years made among us. The waste of wealth, the wreck of worth, the sad fate lighting on the great and good, the vertuous left to scorn, the Loyal us'd as once the *Roman* Parricides: as those in sacks, so these shut under Decks with Cocks and Serpents, desperate and malitious persons left to rule and vex them. Wealth prostituted to the beggarly and the base. Pallaces plundered and pulled down, Temples profan'd, Antiquities raz'd, Religion rivuled into petty Issues running thick corruption.

Probably referring to the disinterment and defilement of Cromwell's body that occurred shortly after the Restoration was announced, Felltham comments: "Then let men consider, after a little Revolu-

tion, how little the Authors gained. Who would take peace from others themselves have miss'd it in their hollow graves; the Earth they tore, hath fled them from her bosome and her Bowels, with nought i'th least considerable to the expence of bloud and treasure."
About the Restoration itself, Felltham is ecstatic: "Then also, let men see, how the Sacred wheel of Providence hath resurrection'd all our joys. How the Church recovers her late besmeared beauties. How the Tide of Trade returns. How brightned Swords have now a peaceful glitter; how Glory, Wealth, and Honour, with Loyalty, is return'd How shouts of joy have drown'd the Cannons Roar; that till men come in Heaven, such joy on Earth can ne're again be expected to be seen."

An analogy indicates that such joy is natural: "So Have I known some generous Courser stand, tremble and quake under both whip and spur; but, once turn'd loose into the open fields, he neighs, curvets, and prances forth his joy; and, gladded now with ease and liberty, he fills himself with pleasure, and all those high contents that bounteous Nature meant him." The closing passage contrasts good order, which is a portion of man's celestial inheritance, with chaos, which is the result of man's sin; peace is included in the angelic portion of man, but war reflects the bestial side: "Certainly, 'tis Peace that makes the world a Paradice; while War, like Sin, does turn it all to Wilderness; and with wild Beasts Mans conversation makes. In War, the vexed Earth abortives all her fruitfulness: but, in an unstirr'd Culture, ripens all her bounties. . . ."

Felltham ends this 1661 essay with a passage from Euripides, a paean to peace:

> Hail lovely *Peace*! thou Spring of wealth,
> Heavens fairest issue, this worlds health.
> O how my Soul does court thy sight?
> More pretious, then the pleasing Light.
> Let never blacker Day appear,
> But dwell, and shine, for ever, here.
> Let shouts of Joy still, still resound:
> While Songs, and Dances walk the round,
> At Feasts of Friends, with Garlands crown'd.

"Of Peace" is not the unseasoned effort of a bookish youngster but the soberly joyous composition of a reflective man. Quotations and allusions abound, but they are informed by personal experience and compassion.

Felltham indeed continued to read in the years between 1628 and 1661; but a list of the works quoted or alluded to in the new and revised essays would be, though expanded, quite similar to that for the excogitations of many years earlier. Significantly, however, Felltham's attitude toward the world about him modified as he grew older. In 1628, he could speak of his own time as "this the crazed age of the World" (L. 29, "That mis-conceit ha's ruin'd Man") and speculate about the decay and imminent end of the world (L. 49, "That all things haue a like progression and fall"). In 1661, however, Felltham asserts "That the present Times are not worse then the Former" (R. S. 76); and he concludes that, "in the general, the World is rather better then worse then it hath been." Although Felltham may still in 1661 be termed a Christian Stoic in such essays as "Of Losses" (R. S. 12), "Of long and short Life" (R. S. 13), " 'Tis neither a great Estate, nor great Honours that can make a man truly Happy" (R. S. 44), "To beware of being Surprised" (R. S. 60), and the long discussion of Ecclesiastes in "Of the use of Pleasure" (R. S. 50), his tone in the Revised Short Century indicates that he sees in his mature years a little less need for a Stoical indifference to the life of this world than he did in 1623 or in 1628.

Felltham began his career in 1623 with a highly specialized prose genre popular at that time, the formal resolve. He ended his career in 1661 with the kind of informal essay that Montaigne had created almost a century earlier. Fortunately, the mature Felltham realized that his genius and cast of mind found their best expression in a genre not formalized, but free; not aloof, but friendly; not detached, but involved. The progressive development of *Resolves* indicates more than one man's changing attitudes toward form and style; it also points to Felltham's important contribution to literary history. The popularity of *Resolves* during the Restoration and the early eighteenth century — and all five editions published between 1661 and 1709 include the Revised Short Century — reasonably suggests that the generosity of spirit; the commonsense approach to the problems of living; the love of the good and full life; and the easy, natural expression found in these last of Felltham's pieces influenced the development of the personal essay in England. If so, Abraham Cowley, Joseph Addison, Richard Steele, Daniel Defoe, Oliver Goldsmith, and even Charles Lamb, William Hazlitt, and Thomas DeQuincey may well owe some debt to this seventeenth-century gentleman of Great Billing, Northamptonshire, who spent his "vacant hours" composing resolves, excogitations, and finally, personal essays.

Owen Felltham's *Resolves: Divine, Morall, Politicall* is an impressive achievement, and one which has not received the critical appreciation it merits. A self-conscious but charitable moralist, Felltham is also a deliberate artist who creates in *Resolves* a work of lasting value. As Laurence Stapleton writes in the most perceptive of recent studies, "The later reader may stimulate his interest in human and humane convictions by turning over the leaves of Felltham. Or he may take more interest in the conscious stylist, expert in pointed sentences and brisk antitheses. But what is most likely to continue Felltham's hold on some favouring readers is his ability, in a sufficient number of his compositions, to link his charitable will, his steady grasp of experience, and his control of statement,"[33] Perhaps Felltham's greatest achievement is to express in a poet's prose an enduring vision of human decency.

CHAPTER 3

A Brief Character
of the Low-Countries

AFTER the introduction of the character genre into England early in the seventeenth century, it was put to a variety of uses and modified accordingly.[1] Originally employed to describe only types of people, the form was very soon expanded to allow the treatment of places. For example, Thomas Dekker sketched prisons and prison life in characters added to the Overburian collection in 1616; and John Earle described "Paules-Walke" and "A Bowle-Alley" in *Microcosmographie*, published in 1628. An additional expansion of the genre, and one in which Felltham played an important role, allowed writers to characterize whole nations.

I *Characters of Nations*

Sir Anthony Weldon, an attendant in the household of King James I during the 1617 progress to Scotland, took what is probably the first step in developing the character of a nation. Disliking everything that he saw in the Northern kingdom, from food to morals, from architecture to personal hygiene, Weldon set down his observations in a brief, vitriolic sketch best known as *A Perfect Description of the People and Country of Scotland*. Imprudent circulation of the little work in manuscript caused Weldon's prompt dismissal from the royal household, and the sketch remained unpublished until 1647 when the Stuart monarchy no longer exerised control over the presses of England.[2]

Although not specifically labeled a "character," Weldon's sketch, running to twenty-one pages in its duodecimo printing, exhibits two important elements of that genre: it generalizes its subject, and it disregards normal principles of organization. Unlike most of the travel literature of the period, *Scotland* presents a generalized impression of an entire country. Weldon constructs a composite picture of "the Scotsman" rather than a series of individual portraits. He belittles "Scottish food" with little reference to specific dishes. Furthermore, his observations on a single subject are not concentrated in a single place within the work; he builds descriptions by scattering the various details of any one topic throughout the sketch. Earlier character writers had found that such organization, though it might seem haphazard, was, in fact, an effective rhetorical device. It forced a careful reading, in one sitting, of the whole work; and it involved the reader in the process of the artistic creation.

Weldon also made significant contributions to the character genre in his *Scotland*. Besides attempting for the first time the characterization of a whole nation and its people, he introduced a style more robust and earthy than any employed by earlier character writers; for he relied in large part on strained, frequently bawdy, metaphor and comic overstatement. When he deplored, for example, the lack of cleanliness among Scottish women of gentle birth, he wrote that "The Ladies are of opinion, that *Susanna* could not be chast, because she bathed so often. Pride is a thing bred in their bones, and their flesh naturally abhors cleanliness; their breath commonly stinks of Pottage, their linen of Piss, their hands of Pigs turds, their body of sweat, and their splay-feet never offend in Socks. To be chained in marriage with one of them, were to be tied to a dead carkass, and cast into a stinking ditch; Formosity [beauty] and a dainty face, are things they dream not of." All subsequent characterizers of nations employ this style.

Despite the historical importance of Weldon's *Scotland*, it did not serve as the ultimate model for the characters of nations which followed. That distinction belongs to Owen Felltham's *A Brief Character of the Low-Countries under the States. Being three weeks observation of the Vices and Vertues of the Inhabitants.* Like Weldon's *Scotland*, Felltham's *Low-Countries* was known to many Englishmen long before it appeared in print. It was occasioned by a trip to the continent which Felltham made between 1623 and 1628, and his work was probably written shortly thereafter.[3] Truncated manuscript copies circulated widely, and at least one found its way to Egypt.[4] In 1648 and again in 1652, the unscrupulous publisher William Ley published unauthorized, abbreviated editions of the work.[5] Later in 1652, Henry Seile, the publisher of *Resolves*, issued for the first time the complete text in an authoritative but anonymous edition. Seile reissued *Low-Countries* in 1659 and again in 1660; and Felltham publicly admitted its authorship in 1661, including it in the *Lusoria* section of the eighth edition of *Resolves*. In

Low-Countries, Felltham followed Weldon's *Scotland* in approach, organization, and style; but he expanded and defined the form. Besides asserting the genre in the title of the work, he enlarged its dimensions to one hundred duodecimo pages and he introduced "Vertues" into the catalogue of "Vices" to give the impression — if not always the fact — of objectivity.

Four other characters of nations appeared after *Low-Countries*, and all show their authors' indebtedness to Felltham. In 1659, the London bookseller John Crooke published *A Character of England* which was supposedly written for a French noble by one of his countrymen but which was actually composed by the diarist John Evelyn. This work was quickly answered by *A Character of France* (1659), an anonymous publication that included an appendix, "Gallus Castratus," which refuted many of the allegations made in *England*. Evelyn answered his critic in an appendix to the third edition of *England* (also 1659); and the bookseller Nathaniel Brooke, who had published *France*, issued in 1660 two additional anonymous characters of nations: *The Character of Italy*, supposedly written by "An English Chyrugion," and *The Character of Spain*. In 1666, one other work appeared which claimed, in its title, to be of the genre, George Alsop's *A Character of the Province of Mary-Land*. Only one-fifth of the book, that chapter dealing with the Susquehanna Indians, is actually a true character; but *Mary-Land* owes much to *Low-Countries*.[6]

II   *The Occasion and Nature of Felltham's Character*

In addition to Felltham's text, all authorized seventeenth-century editions of *Low-Countries* contain a brief, unsigned preface "To the Reader" which was undoubtedly written by Henry Seile. In it, after complaining of the "minc-dmeat" version issued by Ley, Seile explains the occasion of the book's composition and indicates its author's reluctance to publish the work:

long since travelling for companies-sake with a Friend into the Low-Countries, [the author] would needs for his own recreation write this Essay of them as he then found them: I am sure as far from ever thinking to have it publick, as he was from any private spleen to the Nation, or any person in it; for I have moved him often to print it, but could never get his consent, his modesty ever esteeming it among his *puerilla*, and (as he said) a Piece too light for a prudential man to publish: The truth is, it was meerly occasional in his Youth. . . .[7]

The motto of the book is "Non Seria semper," and Felltham may well have had no bitter animosity toward the Dutch when he wrote *Low-Countries;* but the work is highly critical of them in many places. So long as England and Holland were on friendly terms, Seile honored Felltham's expressed wish not to publish the character. But the appearance of Ley's garbled piracies provided a strong argument for issuing a correct version; and in 1652, when war broke out between England and Holland, a good market for anti-Dutch books was created in London. Seile, a good businessman, may have run the risk of "exposing" *Low-Countries* to the book-buying public without its author's "warrant," as he claims in the preface. But Felltham's reluctance to see the work in print was probably not very strong. It was customary for gentlemen authors to promote, in public, the fiction that they scorned publication. In any case, Seile's action seems not to have angered Felltham enough for him to change publishers. Furthermore, by including the character of Holland in the 1661 edition of *Resolves,* Felltham revealed a desire both to see it preserved, light though it might be, and to have it remembered as one of his compositions.

The text of *Low-Countries* is printed in the two parts: the first three-fifths are concerned primarily with the vices of the Dutch; the latter two-fifths are devoted ostensibly to their virtues. When Seile notes this division in his preface, he remarks that, "though the former part be joculary and sportive, yet the seriousness of the later part renders the Character no way injurious to the people." Since his concern not to blacken the reputation of a people with whom the English are at war is no doubt itself "sportive," his statement should not be taken very seriously. His categorizations of the two parts also need modification. The first section is, as he says, primarily descriptive and humorous and the latter is largely historical and reflective. But the first part is not exclusively devoted to vices treated in a witty manner; a few remarks on Dutch virtues are to be found in it, and some of the more serious vices are treated quite soberly. Some humor, likewise, enlivens the second part; and the national traits discussed in it are not wholly admirable. The work as a whole, moreover, is heavily weighted toward the uncomplimentary. Felltham includes only two admirable characteristics in his picture of the Dutch, their industriousness and their martial ability; but he points out numerous faults: gluttony, drunkenness, ostentation, querulousness, and nonconformity, to list but a few. Above all, he scorns their lack of order and degree. Though *Low-Countries* is in many respects quite unlike *Resolves*, the same intellectual and emotional attitudes underlie both works.

III   *Felltham on Holland and the Dutch*

Like any traveler in any age, Felltham was fascinated by the landscape, the housing, the food, the dress, the means of transportation, the language, the occupations, the government, the religion, and other institutions of his hosts, as well as by the traditional subjects of the character, the morality or immorality of the people. All these subjects are treated in *Low-Countries*. In his comments on the landscape and other externals, Felltham combines exaggeration, witty metaphor, and broad humor:

> They are a general Sea-land: the great Bog of *Europe*. There is not such another Marsh in the world, that's flat. They are an universal Quagmire; Epitomiz'd, *A green Cheese in pickle*. There is in them an *Aequilibrium* of mud and water. . . .
> The Soyl is all fat, though wanting the colour to shew it so; for indeed it is the Buttock of the world, full of veins and bloud, but no bones in't. Had S. *Steven* been condemn'd to suffer here, he might have been alive at this day. . . .
> . . . there are Spiders as big as Shrimps, and I think as many. . . .
> The elements are here at variance, the subtile overswaying the grosser; the Fire consumes the Earth, and the Air the Water: they burn Turfs, and drein their grounds with Wind-mills.

There is some praise of the Dutch countryside, but it is undercut in a comparison which suggests affectation: "The Land that they have, they keep as neatly as a Courtier does his Beard. . . ." And there are essentially neutral descriptions, such as the passage on the Dutchman's primary means of transporting goods, which Felltham casts in the form of a riddle: "Their ordinary Pack-horses are all of wood, carry their Bridles in their tails, and their burdens in their bellies. A strong Tyde and a stiff Gale are the spurs that make them speedy: when they travail they touch no ground, and when they stand still they ride, and are never in danger but when they drink up too much of their way."

Felltham uses his description of Dutch houses to comment on two unattractive characteristics of the Dutchman — ostentation and self-satisfaction:

Though their Countrey be part of a main Land, yet every house almost stands in an Island: and that, though a Boor dwell in it, looks as smug as a Lady that hath newly lockt up her Colours, and laid by her Irons. . . .

When you are entred the house, the first thing you encounter is a Looking-glass: No question but a true Embleme of politick hospitality; for though it reflect your self in your own figure, 'tis yet no longer than while you are there before it: when you are gone once, it flatters the next comer, without the least remembrance that you e're were there.

The next are the Vessels of the house, marshalled about the room like Watchmen. . . .

He notices the small paintings hung everywhere, the pride of seventeenth-century Holland; but he dislikes them for one of the reasons that they are now so highly prized, the fact that they picture ordinary life:

Their houses, especially in their Cities are the best eye-beauties of their Countrey: for cost and sight they far exceed our *English*, but they want their magnificence. Their Lining is yet more rich than their out-side, not in Hangings but Pictures, which even the poorest are there furnisht with: Not a Cobler but has his toyes for ornament. Were the knacks of all their houses set together, there would not be such another *Bartholomew-Fair* in *Europe*.

Their Artists for these are as rare as thought, for they can paint you a fat Hen in her feathers. . . .

Any people who take pride in having their ordinary daily life memorialized in paintings must be exceedingly self-satisfied.

Felltham is certainly impressed with the Dutch trait of cleanliness and neatness, but he regards this characteristic as a fault because more important concerns are neglected in striving to maintain outward show: "Every door seems studded with Diamonds. The nails and hinges hold a constant brightnesse, as if rust there were not a quality incident to Iron. Their houses they keep cleaner than their bodies; their bodies than their souls. Go to one, you shall find the Andirons shut up in net-work. At a second, the Warming-pan muffled in Italian Cut-work. At a third the Sconce clad in Cambrick. . . ." Throughout this description of the Dutchman's house, Felltham makes quite explicit his value judgments, and most of them are negative.

As for the typical Dutchman, Felltham finds him to be an exact and therefore an unpleasant combination of what he eats: "His spirits are generated from the *English* Beer, and that makes him head-strong: His body is built of Pickled-Herring, and they render him testy: These with a little Butter, Onyons and *Holland*-Cheese, are the Ingredients of an ordinary *Dutch*-man; which a Voyage to the *East-Indies*, with the heat of the *Aequinoctial,* consolidates." Felltham considers the time that Dutchmen sit at table to be excessive; but he judges the epithet "drunken" — applied to the Dutch for at least a hundred years prior to his visit to Holland — to be less deserved by them than by "your English Gallant." The Dutch, he says, talk too much between drinks to become really drunk.

Of the clothing of his hosts, Felltham concludes: "Their apparel is civil enough and good enough, but very uncomely; and hath usually more stuff than shape." In the 1620s, Englishmen were still using a starch that yellowed their white ruffs and other personal linens, and Felltham is quite obviously startled by the Dutchman's use of bluing in his wash: "Men and Women are there *starched so blew,* that if they once grow old, you would verily believe you saw *Winter* walking up to the neck in a Barrel of *Indigo. . . .*" The Dutch sailor wears "breeches yawning at the knees, as if they were about to swallow his legs unmercifully." And, as for women's fashions, he finds them equally unattractive:

> They are far there from going naked, for of a whole woman you can see but half a face. As for her hand, that shews her a sore Labourer; which you shall ever find as it were in recompence loaden with Rings to the cracking of her fingers. If you look lower, She's a Monkey chain'd about the middle, and had rather want it in dyet, than not have silver-links to hang her keyes in.
>
> Their Gowns are fit to hide great Bellies, but they make them shew so unhandsome that men do not care for getting them. Marry this you shall find to their commendation, their smocks are ever whiter than their skin.

This criticism of the Dutch is somewhat relieved by the inclusion of two points in their favor, the modesty of their women and the cleanliness of their clothing; but each of these virtures is almost immediately compromised.

Among the Dutch institutions, Felltham finds the two most important ones, the church and the temporal state, worthy of scorn. He despises both a sanctioned proliferation of religious sects and a democratic form of government. Complaining that "all strange Religions throng thither," he concludes:

> 'Tis an University of all Religions, which grow here confusedly (like stocks in a Nursery) without either order or pruning. If you be unsetled in your

Religion, you may here try all, and take at last what you like best. If you fancy none, you have a pattern to follow of two that would be a Church by themselves.

'Tis the Fair of all the Sects, where all the Pedlers of Religion have leave to vent their toyes, their Ribbands, and Phanatick Rattles. And should it be true, it were a cruel brand which *Romists* stick upon them; for (say they) as the *Chameleon* changes into all colours but white, so they admit of all Religions but the true: For the *Papist* onely may not exercise his in publick; yet his restraint they plead is not in hatred but justice, because the *Spaniard* abridges the *Protestant:* and they had rather shew a little spleen, than not cry quit with their enemy. His act is their warrant, which they retaliate justly. . . .

Now albeit the *Papist* do them wrong herein, yet can it not excuse their boundless Toleration, which shews they place their Republick in a higher esteem than Heaven it self; and had rather cross upon God than it. For whosoever disturbs the Civil Government is lyable to punishment; but the Decrees of Heaven and Sanctions of the Deity, any one may break uncheck'd, by professing what false Religion he please.

Perhaps Felltham is overreacting to the freedom of worship in Holland; certainly the religious toleration expressed in *Resolves* is missing in this raillery. Yet it should be remembered that Felltham advocated a toleration of belief within a state church, not a multitude of independent sects. And, too, Holland opened its cities in the early seventeenth century to those Englishmen who were such rabid Separatists that they could not live in peace at home or allow their neighbors to do so. Felltham views religious divisiveness, therefore, as a potential cause of civil chaos.

The democratic Dutch state itself is subjected to the conservative young Royalist's abuse: "The Countreys government is a Democracy, and there had need be many to rule such a Rabble of rude ones. Tell them of a King, and they could cut your throat in earnest: the very name carries servitude in it, and they hate it more than a *Jew* doth Images, a woman old age, or a Non-conformist a Surplice." This felicitous trio of comparisons is followed by an attack on those who have been elected to positions of authority in the government: "None among them hath Authority by inheritance, that were the way in time to parcel out their Countrey to Families. They are chosen all as our Kings chuse Sheriffs for the Counties; not for their sin of wit, but for the wealth they have to bear it out withall; which they so over-affect, that *Myn Here* shall walk the streets as Usurers go to Baudy-houses, all alone and melancholy. . . . A common voice hath given him preeminence, and he loses it by living as he did when he was but a Boor."

Since this Dutch passion for democracy is carried into their homes, Felltham complains of the lack of authority and respect found in them:

> In their Families they all are equals, and you have no way to know the Master and Mistress, but by taking them in bed together: It may be those are they; otherwise *Malky* [the servant girl] can prate as much, laugh as loud, be as bold, and sit as well as her Mistress.
>
> Had *Logicians* lived here first, Father and Son had never passed so long for Relatives. They are here Individuals, for no Demonstrance of Duty or Authority can distinguish them, as if they were created together, and not born successively. . . .
>
> Your man shall be saucy, and you must not strike; if you do, he shall complain to the *Schout*, and perhaps have recompence. 'Tis a dainty place to please boyes in: for your Father shall bargain with your School-master not to whip you: if he doth, he shall revenge it with his knife, and have Law for it.

Complete democracy, Felltham concludes, ultimately violates the principle of order and degree. By virtue of age, wisdom, or position, certain individuals should have the right to exercise more authority than others.

In addition to boorishness Felltham finds in the Dutch character querulousness and savagery, selfishness and love of gain. "You may sooner convert a *Iew*, than make an ordinary *Dutch-man* yield to Arguments that cross him. . . ." "For their condition they are Churlish as their breeder *Neptune;* and without doubt very ancient, for they were bred before Manners were in fashion." "They should make good Justices, for they respect neither persons nor apparel. . . ." As might be expected, the Dutchman takes offence at anyone's pointing out his faults: "Nothing can quiet them but money and liberty, yet when they have them, they abuse both; but if you tell them so, you awake their fury, and you may sooner calm the Sea than conjure that into compass again. Their anger hath no eyes, and their judgement doth not flow so much from reason as passion and partiality."

In war, they are extremely savage:

> 'Tis their own Chronicle business, which can tell you, that at the Siege of *Leyden*, a Fort being held by the *Spanish*, by the *Dutch* was after taken by Assault; the Defendants were put to the Sword, where one of the *Dutch* in

the fury of the slaughter ript up the Captains body, and with a barbarous
hand tore out the yet living heart, panting among the reeking bowels, then
with his teeth rent it still warm with bloud into gobbets, which he spitted
over the Battlements in defiance to the rest of the Army.

Oh Tigers breed! the *Scythian* Bear could ne're have been more savage:
To be necessitated into cruelty, is a misfortune to the strongly tempted to it;
but to let spleen rave and mad it in resistless bloud, shews nature steep'd i'th
livid gall of passion, and beyond all brutishnesse displayes the un-noble
tyranny of a prevailing Coward.

And Felltham remarks, concerning the Hollander's selfishness and
passion for money, that "They love none but those that do for them,
and when they leave off they neglect them." "Their justice is strict if
it cross not policy: but rather than hinder Traffique, tolerates any
thing."

Such are the vices that Felltham finds in the Dutch: self-
satisfaction, ostentation, total independence in matters of religion
and government, boorishness, querulousness, savagery, selfishness,
and love of gain. The only characteristics shown to mitigate even
slightly these faults are neatness, cleanliness, and modesty; and the
areas in which these virtues are manifest often betray a misplaced
sense of values.

Felltham organizes "a Fairer Object" — his consideration of
Dutch virtues — around Proverbs 30:24-28, wherein "Solomon tells
of four things that are small and full of wisdom, the Pismire, the
Grass-hopper, the Coney, and the Spider." The Dutch are compared
in turn to each of these small creatures. Ants make provisions for the
future by storing in the summer the food needed for the long winter
that follows. The Dutch, who

have nothing but what grass affords them, are yet, for almost all provisions
the Store-house of the whole of *Christendom*. What is it which there may
not be found in plenty? they making by their industry all the fruits of the
vast Earth their own. What Land can boast a privilege that they do not par-
take of? They have not of their own enough materials to compile one ship,
yet how many Nations do they furnish? The remoter angles of the world do
by their pains deliver them their sweets; and bring of themselves in want,
their diligence hath made them both *Indies* nearer home.

They are frugal to the saving of Egge-shells, and maintain it for a Maxim,
that a thing lasts longer mended than new.

Their Cities are their Mole-hills; their *Schutes* and *Fly-boats* creep and
return with their store for Winter. Every one is busie, and carries his grain;
as if every City were a several *Hive*, and the *Bees* not permitting a Drone to

inhabit; for idle persons must find some other mansion. And lest necessity bereave men of means to set them on work, there are publick Banks, that (without use) lend upon pawns to all the poor that want.

The Dutchman's industry is not an unmixed blessing, however, since it breeds a provincial outlook and craftiness:

they look upon others too little, and upon themselves too much; And wheresoever they light in a pleasant or rich soyl, like suckers and lower plants, they rob from the root of that Tree which gives them shade and protection; so their wisdom is not indeed Heroick or Numinal, as courting an univeral good; but rather narrow and restrictive, as being a wisdom but for themselves. Which, to speak plainly, is descending into Craft; and is but the sinister part of that which is really Noble and Coelestial.

The author of Proverbs praises the wisdom of the rabbit in making its home among the rocks, a place relatively safe from its enemies. Though their enemies, the Spanish, are all about them, the Dutch "rest secure in their own inescapable Berries. Where have you under Heaven, such impregnable Fortifications? Where Art beautifies Nature, and Nature makes Art invincible. . . ." Indeed, some of these great fortifications are still preserved in the cities of The Netherlands. Felltham draws one contrast between the Dutch and the animals they seem to have imitated: "The Conies find Rocks, and they make them."

Locusts deserve praise, says the author of Proverbs, since, having no king, they recognize the necessity to go about in bands. In war, says Felltham, the Dutch "are Grasse-hoppers, and without a King, go forth in bands to conquer Kings. They have not only defended themselves at their own home, but have braved the *Spaniard* at his." After giving examples of this latter statement — the taking of the Grand Canary Island in 1599 and the Dutch defeat of the Spanish fleet at Gibraltar in 1607 — he concludes that

There hardly is upon earth such a school of Martiall Discipline. 'Tis the Christian worlds *Academy* for Arms; whither all the neighbour-Nations resort to be instructed; where they may observe how unresistible a blow many small grains of powder will make, being heaped together, which yet if you separate, can do nothing but sparkle and die.

Their recreation is the practise of Arms; And they learn to be souldiers sooner than men. Nay, as if they placed a Religion in Arms, every Sunday is concluded with the Train'd-Bands marching through their Cities.

Felltham certainly praises here the Dutchman's warlike spirit, which he had earlier decried. What he undoubtedly means is that when there is external danger, a bellicose spirit is admirable; but such a spirit is intolerable when men are at home and among friends.

In Proverbs, the spider is praised for making her home with her own hands; for the same reason Felltham admires the Dutch:

> Even among us, they shame us with their industry, which makes them seem as if they had a faculty from the worlds Creation, out of water to make dry land appear. They win our drowned grounds which we cannot recover, and chase back *Neptune* to his own old Banks.
>
> All that they do is by such labour as it seems extracted out of their own bowels. And in their wary thrift, they hang by such a slender sustenation of life, that one would think their own weight should be enough to crack it. Want of Idleness keeps them from want. And 'tis their Diligence makes them Rich.

No one in Holland — Dutchman or foreigner — is allowed to go in want. Work is provided for the unemployed, good hospitals for those unable to work, and decent asylums for the insane.

When Felltham speculates about what occasioned the industriousness of these people, he thinks that their eagerness to work may be a response to "the nature of their Country, in which if they be not laborious they cannot live"; or it may be the result of "an Innate Genius of the people by a Superiour Providence." In either case, the result has made the Dutch "in some sort Gods, for they set bounds to the Sea, and when they list let it pass them. Even their dwelling is a miracle; They live lower than the fishes in the very lap of the floods, and incircled in their watry Arms. They are the *Israelites* passing through the Red-Sea. The waters wall them in, and if they set open their sluces shall drown up their enemies."

With Biblical parallels and comparisons drawn from natural history, Felltham praises the Dutch for their military accomplishments against England's old enemy:

> They have strugled long with *Spains Pharaoh*, and they have at length inforced him to let them go. They are a *Gideons* Army upon the march again. They are the *Indian* Rat, gnawing the bowels of the *Spanish Crocadile*, to which they got when he gap'd to swallow them. They are a serpent wreathed about the legs of that *Elephant*. They are the little sword-fish pricking the bellies of the *Whale*. They are the wane of that Empire, which increas'd in *Isabella*, and in *Charls* the 5th. was at full.

Rulers who disregard the rights of their subjects, as the Spanish did in trying to force Roman Catholicism on the staunchly Protestant Dutch, should take note. The Dutch

are a glass wherein Kings may see, that though they be Soveraigns over lives and goods, yet when they usurp upon Gods part, and will be Kings over conscience too, they are sometimes punisht with losse of that which lawfully is their own. That Religion too fiercely urg'd, is to stretch a string till it not onely jars but cracks, and in the breaking whips (perhaps) the streiners eye out.

That an extreme Taxation is to take away the honey while the Bees keep the Hive; whereas he that would take that, should first either burn them or drive them out. That Tyrants in their Government, are the greatest Traitors to their own Estates. That a desire of being too absolute, is to walk upon Pinacles and the tops of *Pyramides*, where not onely the footing is full of hazard, but even the sharpness of that they tread on may run into their foot and wound them. That too much to regrate on the patience of but tickle Subjects, is to press a Thorn till it prick your finger. That nothing makes a more desperate Rebel than a Prerogative inforced too far.

This passage receives special attention in Benjamin Boyce's study of the polemic character. Noting that *A Brief Character of the Low-Countries* was first printed in 1652, the year in which England entered into open war with Holland, Boyce speculates that these sentiments concerning the limitation of kingship are not Felltham's but were "inserted by an Amsterdamnified publisher. . . ."[8] William Ley's pirated version of the character, appearing four years before the war with Holland, has this particular passage; Seile, then, could hardly be the "Amsterdamnified publisher" responsible for it. On the other hand, Ley cannot seriously be considered as the author of the passage; for Felltham would not have allowed in the authorized edition of his character any materials plagiarized from a pirated one. It must be concluded, therefore, that Felltham wrote the passage himself.

Moreover, this warning to rulers who overstep their prerogative is easily reconciled with Felltham's often-expressed reverence for the crown: he is writing about the Spanish king, not the English one. Since the mid-sixteenth century, the English had looked on the Spanish monarch as second only to the Pope in evil intentions toward England and as greater than the Pope in the ability to carry out those intentions. Spain commanded large armies and, of greater threat to England's security, large navies. Quite naturally, then,

Felltham takes this opportunity to praise the Dutch for resisting the Spanish and, especially, to warn this and future Spanish kings against trying to force Roman Catholicism upon unwilling peoples. That this warning to Spain's king, probably written before 1628, parallels somewhat the arguments used later by the English Puritans to justify the execution of their monarch Charles I is ironic rather than prophetic. The most tenable conclusion is that Felltham, while very much in favor of a monarchical form of government, was not a blind worshipper of kingship. He knows that individual kings, being merely men, are subject to human frailty; and he points out the faults of a bad king, not realizing that twenty years later his beloved Charles would be accused of the same faults.

Felltham notes one other Dutch virtue, an honesty in the manufacture and the sale of goods; and he discusses with some admiration their language ("as old as *Babel*"), their history (with liberal reliance on Tacitus), and their gross annual product (over twice that of England). He concludes *Low-Countries* with a play on the microcosm-macrocosm analogy so common in the Renaissance. The Dutch personality seems filled with contradictions, but

If any man wonder at these Contraries, let him look in his own body for as many several humours, in his own Brain for as many different fancies, in his own Heart for as various passions; and from all these he may learn, That *There is not in all the World such another Beast as MAN.*

The author of *Resolves* concentrates on man's spiritual potential; the author of *A Brief Character of the Low-Countries* focuses on baser stuff. But the same concept of what man can and should be underlies both works, and each is in its own way moral and didactic.

While the tone of this little character book is considerably lighter than that of *Resolves*, permitting more extravagant — at times even outrageous — play with language, the elements of style evident here are much the same as those seen in the earlier two centuries of *Resolves:* a fondness for aphoristic statement, the metaphorical use of words, and the telling illustration and example. Certainly, too, the alternation between playfulness and seriousness in style suits the frequent shifting from trivial to serious matters. The lightness and humor present in so much of the work should not mislead the reader into thinking that *Low-Countries* is all youthful exuberance; much of it is concerned with one of Felltham's favorite serious themes: the Dutch are time and again criticized because they lack order, degree, and moderation in their private lives, their family relationships, their churches, and their state. Even when writing a sportive sketch in his youth, the moralizer of *Resolves* would not, or could not, completely ignore his most deeply felt convictions.

A Brief Character of the Low-Countries is interesting in and of itself; and it certainly deserves more attention than it has so far received. It merits study as a pioneer in a genre that provided much of the impetus for subsequent works written to characterize nations and peoples; as a social and historical document that gives valuable insight into what a conservative English tourist in the earlier seventeenth century thought of one of England's most important neighbors; and as a piece of playful literature that is a good example of some of the wilder flights of wit and humor that seventeenth-century prose could produce. Finally, as a part of Felltham's canon, *Low-Countries* is important in showing, more clearly than *Resolves*, that this grave moralist could be — when the occasion presented itself — as sportive and as provocative as anyone; and this varied capability rounds out the man and his work.

CHAPTER 4

The Poetry

OWEN Felltham, recognized by Anthony à Wood as one of the poets "which were the chiefest of the Nation" in the 1630s,[1] is, ironically, represented quite sparingly in modern anthologies of seventeenth-century verse and is almost totally neglected by modern critics. It is to be hoped that a recent edition of his poems,[2] the only complete collection ever attempted, may reawaken interest in Felltham as a poet. Fewer than fifty poems recognized as his survive, but this small canon is distinguished. In his thirty-one occasional pieces, Felltham provides some stimulating and frequently moving tributes, elegies, epitaphs, and reflective poems. In his lyrics, the author of *Resolves* offers some of the most charming love poems of the period; indeed, a few of them are among the best metaphysical poems on that subject after Donne's.

I *Poems on Literary Figures and Subjects*

Felltham's verses about literary men and their works are interesting for what they tell of the poet himself — his interests, his prejudices, his critical insights. Felltham's first published poem, "Authori," prefaced to Kingsmill Long's translation of John Barclay's *Argenis* (1625), has little interest except for such information. *Argenis*, originally published in Latin in 1621, is a didactic courtly romance containing political allegory; and Felltham finds the book appropriate "When I would read for *pleasure*, or to spy/*Wisdome*, with *Worth*, and *State-Philosophy*. . . ." Aside from this couplet, the poem chiefly praises not the author of *Argenis* but its translator for having "naturaliz'd" the work. Because of Long's ability, the book now "doth in *English* reigne. . . ."

At this time Felltham was probably working on the essays published in 1628 as the second century of *Resolves*; these pieces contain many passages of Classical poetry — some quite brief, others rather lengthy — to which he appended his own translations. As a result, Felltham knew firsthand the problem of the translator. Since ". . . Bookes translated, doe, like Silke/Twice dy'de, lose glosse. . . ," the translator must "provide a various dresse, and fit/That to anothers Childe. . . ." These two effective metaphors unite in Felltham's statement that, though "changing [the] colour" of *Argenis*, Long's translation "keep'st the beauty still." Thus Felltham displays early in his poetic career his skill at finding and using apt imagery, even in a poem written about the most pedestrian of subjects.

Two of the most colorful patrons of literature and other arts in the earlier seventeenth century were Sir Kenelm Digby and his wife Venetia Stanley. Venetia, whom Ben Jonson enthroned as his Muse,[3] was one of the most celebrated beauties of her day. She was not known for her morality, however; rumor had it that she had given birth to at least one bastard. When she died under mysterious circumstances on 1 May 1633, "The curious and loose-tongued spread abroad the word that Kenelm had killed her by having her eat capons fed on wine of vipers. His intention, they said, was thus to preserve her beauty."[4] Sir Kenelm spent much effort in denying these rumors; he explained that Venetia was accustomed to taking viper wine to relieve her frequent headaches. The vicious talk grew so prevalent that King Charles ordered an autopsy performed, and the examination showed that Venetia's brain was "much putrefied and corrupted."[5]

Probably a friend of the couple, Felltham sought to answer these charges in a poem descriptively entitled "*Funebre Venetianum.* On the Lady Venetia Digby, found dead in her bed, leaning her head on her hand." Felltham attacks the gossip mongers on two counts. First, to those who condemned Venetia's morals and to those who accused Sir Kenelm of having murdered her, he warns: "Rash Censure stay: nor he, nor she that's gone/Must be condemnd: unless to *Jove* alone/Fate's folded up. . . ." Then, almost grotesquely punning on the results of the autopsy, he confutes those who, "striving to salve their own/Deep want of skill, have in a fury thrown/Scandal on her, and say she wanted brain."

He asks how Venetia could have captivated wise men had she not been possessed of the highest intelligence. Her mind, Felltham says, was of such a high order that death came as respectfully to her as would a man paying court:

> this was it
> Which made death mannerly, and strive to fit
> Himself with reverence to her; that now
> He came not like a Tyrant, on whose brow
> A pompous terrour hung; but in a strain
> Lovely and calm, as is the *June* serain [serene]
> That now, who most abhor him can but say,
> Gently he did imbrace her into clay:
> And her, as Monument for time to come,
> Left her own statue, perfect for her tomb.

Despite this clever and lovely view of Venetia's death, certainly a passage in which Felltham accomplishes a high order of art, the poem as a whole is not one of Felltham's most successful. The organization is loose; and the work suffers from a lack of unity in that its two distinct intents do not merge successfully: the defense of Sir Kenelm and Venetia, and the praise of Venetia. The consolatory ending, for all its beauty and power, is also somewhat unsatisfying in the context of the poem's occasion and title.

Sometime during the late 1620s or the early 1630s Thomas Randolph, a facile and witty young poet, wrote a poem praising Felltham and his *Resolves*. Although the two men did not know each other at the time (line 35 of Randolph's poem reads: "th' art unknown to me"), they were soon to meet and become friends. Randolph died in 1635 at the age of thirty, and three years later a posthumous volume of his works was published, *Poems with the Mvses Looking-Glasse: And amyntas*. Felltham contributed to it an elegiac and commendatory poem "On his beloved friend the Author, and his ingenious Poems." This lengthy piece, consisting of fortyseven heroic couplets, begins with a conventional statement which Felltham, through his choice of metaphor and image, makes fresh:

> What need these busy wits? who hath a Mine
> His owne, thus rich, needs not the scatter'd shine
> Of lesser heapes: Day dimmes a taper's light:
> And lamps are uselesse, where there is no night.

This deprecation of commendatory verse leads into another convention — to the statement that the dead poet's own work is his best memorial:

> Why then this traine of writers? forreigne verse
> Can adde no honour to a Poet's hearse,

> Whose every line, which he to paper lent,
> Builds for himselfe a lasting Monument.
> Brave verse this priviledge hath; Though all be dumbe
> That is the Authors Epitaph and Tombe.

After making this statement, however, Felltham probably found himself in a dilemma. He evidently liked Randolph very much; yet while he sincerely wished to praise Randolph's poetry, he clearly could find little of real substance to admire in the young man's work. He overcame the problem by praising the facility with which Randolph wrote:

> Such was his *Genius:* Like the eyes quick wink;
> Hee could write sooner, then an other think.
> His play was Fancies flame, a lightning wit,
> So shot, that it could sooner pierce, then hit.

Randolph was also skillful in making what he wrote believable: "What e're he pleas'd, though but in sport to prove,/Appear'd as true. . . ." Without reviewing Randolph's actual accomplishments, Felltham imagines what this young poet might have been able to achieve had he lived longer:

> Had hee
> Liv'd but with us, till grave maturity;
> Though wee should ever in his change have lost,
> Wee might have gaind enough whereof to boast
> Our nations better Genius; But now
> Our hopes are nipt, e're they began to blow.

The poem concludes with a restatement of the one thing that Felltham could find to praise without reservation: no one else but Randolph "could so quickly, doe so much, so well."

Felltham's reticence in his praise of Randolph is striking when this poem is read with others published in *Poems with the Mvses Looking-Glasse.* Other poets writing commendatory verses for that same volume rank Randolph with Jonson and Shakespeare. Significantly, modern critics such as Douglas Bush have concurred in Felltham's judgment: "The pastoral, erotic, and festive verse of the short-lived and much-praised Thomas Randolph . . . was rather too facile and unoriginal. . . ; among the courtly and metaphysical poets he remained the precocious undergraduate. . . ."[6] The anthologists Alexander Witherspoon and Frank Warnke comment in their headnote to two of Randolph's poems that, "Exorbitantly admired in his own day, the short-lived Thomas Randolph has not attracted the attention of posterity to any great degree. His poems and plays have their share of the wit and charm common to the school of Jonson, but they lack an individual note, any of that 'unexpressible addition of comeliness' which makes unforgettable so much seventeenth-century literature. . . ."[7]

Randolph's mentor and adoptive father, Ben Jonson, is undoubtedly the most important literary figure that Felltham knew personally; and two of his poems concern that great dramatist. The first one, "An Answer to the Ode of Come leave the loathed Stage," is a playful, occasionally biting piece written in response to one of Jonson's poetical tirades; the second, "To the Memory of immortal Ben," is a moving and informed tribute composed to mourn Jonson's death.

In 1629, Jonson's comedy *The New Inn* was, as Jonson complained on the title page of the 1631 edition of the play, "most negligently play'd by some the Kings Seruants. And more squeamishly beheld, and censured by others, the Kings Subiects."[8] Disgusted by the reception of his effort, Jonson wrote an "Ode to himselfe,"[9] which begins:

> Come leaue the lothed stage,
> And the more lothsome age:
> Where pride, and impudence (in faction knit)
> Vsurpe the chaire of wit!

Jonson vows to

> Leaue things so prostitute,
> And take the *Alcaick* Lute;
> Or thine owne *Horace*, or *Anacreons* Lyre;
> Warme thee, by *Pindares* fire. . . .

Obviously smarting under censure, Jonson boasts that, though he may be physically infirm, he is still able to write poetry that will force the curious and the envious to blush and "sweare no palsey's in thy braine."

Jonson's "Ode" called forth some laudatory replies in verse; the most notable among these poems are by Randolph and Carew. But, as Gerard Langbaine comments in his *English Dramatic Poets*, " 'Twas great pity, that he that was so great a Master in

Poetry, should not retain that old Axiom in *Morality, Nosce Teip-sum*. . . . He had then prevented that sharp reply made by the Ingenious Mr. *Feltham*, to this Magisterial Ode. . . ."[10] Felltham's reply, known variously as "Against Ben: Johnson" and as "An Answer to the Ode of Come leave the loathed Stage, &c.," is certainly ingenious and witty. Significantly, it also contains, as Herford and Simpson remark, "some very just criticism."[11]

Imitating quite closely the form of Jonson's poem, Felltham accuses the playwright not only of bad temper but also of loss of his powers: "Come leave this saucy way/Of baiting those that pay/Dear for the sight of your declining wit. . . ." He turns Jonson's remarks about pride and impudence against the dramatist himself:

> I wonder by what Dowre
> Or Patent you had power
> From all to rap't a judgment. Let't suffice,
> Had you been modest, y'had been granted wise.

To Jonson's complaint in his ode that the audience wants only "some mouldy tale" reworked, Felltham retorts that Jonson is incapable of true invention:

> 'Tis known you can do well,
> And that you do excell
> As a translator: But when things require
> A *genius* and fire,
> Not kindled heretofore by others pains;
> As oft y'have wanted brains
> And art to strike the White,
> As you have levell'd right:
> Yet if men vouch not things Apocryphal
> You bellow, rave and spatter round your gall.

Jonson gives as an example of a "mouldy tale" *Pericles*, undoubtedly referring to the play attributed at least in part to Shakespeare. Felltham turns Jonson's criticism back in a three-fold attack. He criticizes some of the low characters in *The New Inn;* he complains about the play's absurd plot; and, strange to see in a commentary about a drama by Ben Jonson, he points out a violation of decorum:

> *Jug, Pierce, Peck, Fly,* and all
> Your Jests so nominal,
> Are things so far beneath an able Brain,

> As they do throw a stain
> Through all th'unlikely plot, and do displease
> As deep as *Pericles*,
> Where yet there is not laid
> Before a Chamber-maid
> Discourse so weigh'd, as might have serv'd of old
> For Schools, when they of Love and Valour told.

Violation of decorum is certainly present in Jonson's drama; for he has Prudence, a lady's maid, set up as sovereign of the sports to preside over a court of love in which a gentleman wins a lady by discoursing learnedly and wittily on the subjects of love and valor (act 3, sc. 2 and act 4, sc. 4).

Jonson scorns the critics of his play as "Braue *plush*, and *veluet-men*" fit to feed only on the scraps of a meal; but Felltham asserts that even these can judge aright:

> Why Rage then? when the show
> Should Judgment be and Know-
> ledge, that there are in Plush who scorn to drudge,
> For Stages yet can judge
> Not only Poets looser lines but wits,
> And all their Perquisits.

Langbaine notes of Felltham's treatment of "Knowledge" that "This Break was purposely design'd by the Poet to ape that in Ben's third Stanza" (in the word "fish-scraps").[12]

Jonson concludes his poem by vowing to write henceforth only light lyrics and poetry that praises King Charles. Felltham calls for modesty, but he commends in the last couplet of his "Answer" both Jonson and his prospective theme, the King:

> *Alcaeus* Lute had none,
> Nor loose *Anacreon*
> E're taught so bold assuming of the Bayes,
> When they deserv'd no praise.
> To rail men into approbation
> Is new, is yours alone,
> And prospers not: For know
> Fame is as coy as you
> Can be disdainful; and who dares to prove
> A rape on her, shall gather scorn, not love.

Leave then this humour vain,
And this more humorous strain,
Where self-conceit and choler of the bloud
Eclipse what else is good:
Then if you please those raptures high to touch
Whereof you boast so much;
And but forbear your Crown
Till the world puts it on:
No doubt from all you may amazement draw,
Since braver Theme no *Phoebus* ever saw.

Some of Jonson's partisans criticize Felltham's "Answer" as cruel. John Palmer, for instance, comments: "To his shame Owen Felltham, author of *The Resolve* [sic], expressed the feeling of the town in a parody which in the circumstances was ungenerous. . . . deserting his master at this unhappy moment."[13] The more judicious Larry S. Champion refers to Felltham's parody as sarcastic.[14] Even Herford and Simpson, who have made probably the truest estimate of Felltham's "Answer," seemingly fail to see the humor in the poem: "Feltham's retort is a not unfair rebuke to a great man who had tried to capture fortune by violence; and his survey of Jonson's achievements, though grudging, allows that he had 'hit the white' as often as not."[15] Felltham's praise of Jonson is not grudging; indeed, the nature of his poem indicates that as parodist he is simply having great fun with the immediate situation and that he actually does admire Jonson's great achievements. The very wit and playfulness of the "Answer" preclude any real ill-feeling. No evidence that Jonson took offense at the poem exists, and Felltham's final tribute to the playwright is one of sincere and judicious praise.

Jonson died in 1637 and was buried in Westminster Abbey. The following year Henry Seile, Felltham's publisher, issued *Ionsonvs Virbivs*, a volume of thirty-three elegies written about the great dramatist by such poets and playwrights as William Cartwright, Lord Falkland, John Ford, Sidney Godolphin, James Howell, Henry King, and Edmund Waller. In this collection, Owen Felltham's "To the Memory of immortall Ben," a seventy-four-line poem in heroic couplets, appeared. Felltham lists Jonson's best qualities, saying that as playwright and poet this giant combined the best of all ancient models:

when the World shall know, that *Pindar*'s height,
Plautus his wit, and *Seneca*'s grave weight,

> *Horace* his matchlesse Nerves, and that high phrase
> Wherewith great *Lucan* doth his Readers maze,
> Shall with such radiant illustration glide,
> (As if each line to life were property'd)
> Through all thy Workes; And like a Torrent move,
> Rowling the *Muses* to the Court of *Jove,*
> Wits generall Tribe, will soone intitle thee
> Heire to *Apollo's* ever verdant Tree.

Undoubtedly alluding to the poorly received plays of Jonson's last years, among them *The New Inn,* Felltham comments that " 'twill by all concluded be, the Stage/Is widowed now; was bed-rid by thy age." Nevertheless, the period in which Jonson reigned with all his powers will in the future be compared to Rome's golden age:

> Aswell as Empire, wit his Zenith hath,
> Nor can the rage of time, or tyrants wrath
> Encloud so bright a flame: But it will shine
> In spight of envie, till it grow divine.
> As when *Augustus* raign'd, and warre did cease,
> *Romes* bravest wits were usher'd in by peace:
> So in our Halcyon dayes, we have had now
> Wits, to which, all that after come, must bow.

This statement is one of the earliest acknowledgments of the greatness of Elizabethan and Jacobean drama, and in it Felltham assigns special places of honor to three gifted dramatists:

> And should that Stage compose her selfe a Crowne
> Of all those wits, which hitherto sh'as knowne:
> Though there be many that about her brow
> Like sparkling stones, might a quick lustre throw:
> Yet, *Shakespeare, Beaumont, Johnson,* these three shall
> Make up the Jem in the point Verticall.

Shakespeare's place in the crown's apex can be understood, although 1638 is rather early in the history of his adulation. Jonson's place is also defensible not only because this poem is intended to celebrate his achievement but also because his worth as a playwright and a poet is widely recognized. The inclusion of Beaumont is, however, something of a surprise to the modern reader unless he realizes the great esteem in which that dramatist — the first playwright to be buried in Westminster Abbey[16] — was held in the 1620s and 1630s.

Felltham continues his tribute to Jonson by remarking on the critical dicta for which that playwright is probably best noted:

> And now since JOHNSON'S gone, we well may say,
> The stage hath seen her glory and decay.
> Whose judgement was't refined it? Or who
> Gave Lawes, by which hereafter all must goe.
> But solid JOHNSON?

And Felltham praises Jonson for what amounts to the Senecanism of his style: "from whose full strong quill/Each line did like a Diamond drop distill,/Though hard, yet cleare." After praising *Sejanus* and *Catiline*, Felltham considers Jonson's most frequently cited fault; but, in the process, he turns it into a virtue:

> Admit his Muse was slow. 'Tis Judgements Fate
> To move, like greatest Princes, still in state.
> Those Planets placed in the higher Sphœres,
> End not their motion but in many yeares;
> Whereas light *Venus* and the giddy Moone,
> In one or some few dayes their courses run.
> Slow are substantial bodies. . . .
> . . . .
>   every line
> Must be considered, where men spring a mine.
> And to write things that Time can never staine,
> Will require sweat, and rubbing of the braine.

Felltham concludes the poem by admitting that any attempt of his to praise Jonson has been precluded: "He/Of whom I write this, has prevented me,/And boldly said so much in his owne praise,/No other pen need any Trophie raise." The eighteenth-century enemy of Jonson, Edmund Malone, misinterpreted Felltham's remark, perhaps purposely, citing it as proof that Jonson did not trust to the plaudits of others but frequently wrote in praise of himself.[17] William Gifford in his edition of Jonson correctly interprets the passage in question: "The *praise* refers to our author's works. It is in the composition of his *Sejanus, Cataline*, and other poems mentioned by Feltham that he pronounces Jonson to have said so much in his own praise as to make the applause of his friends superfluous. . . ."[18]

Felltham's "To the Memory of immortal Ben" is a considerable achievement. The poem stands as further testimony to the critical in-

sight Felltham displayed in his poem on Randolph and in his
"Answer": he recognizes the greatness of the early seventeenth-
century drama and the supremacy of Shakespeare and Jonson. But,
more importantly, the poem succeeds as a convincing and sincere
tribute to the dead playwright. Its success lies in its careful construc-
tion, its deft use of biography and convention, and its beauty of
language. "To the Memory of immortal Ben" is the best of
Felltham's occasional poems on literary figures, and it certainly must
rank among the most distinguished tributes Jonson received.

II   Poems on Political and Religious
Figures and Subjects

Felltham's earliest poem that commemorates a political figure is
probably "Elegie on Henry Earl of Oxford." Henry de Vere, born in
1593, led a profligate youth; but he became a national hero in 1625
when he died of a fever while fighting for the Dutch. Felltham's
poem contains an attack on "dull *Holland*," which, having no
worthy men herself, offers up to Fate this English nobleman,
"Whose every Limb was worth more than thy state." In lines which
are metaphysical in their complex thought patterns and striking
metaphor, the poet, still addressing Holland, laments Oxford's
death:

> I know the gods are pleas'd with't, but 'tis we
> That feel the losse, not they, nor you, nor he.
> Heaven joyes in his accesse, and he in that:
> And you thought so much good might expiate
> Your blackest sins: not thinking we should be,
> Like low Orbes wanting *Primum Mobile*.

Comparing Oxford to Sir Philip Sidney, who had died in the Low
Countries under similar circumstances almost forty years earlier,
Felltham asserts that

> Great Vertues have this Grant, they never dye,
> But like Time live to kisse Eternity.
> And now men doubt which Name can cite a tear,
> Or make a Souldier first, *Sidney* or *Vere*.

The poem concludes with a warning to Holland not to let the Earl of
Oxford's place of death be known,

> lest when men see
> His worth, and come to know he dy'd for thee
> They curse thee lower than thy staple, Fish;
> Thy own Beer-drinkers, or the *Spaniards* wish.
> But if by curious search it must be known,
> Write by it thus, *Here* Belgia *was undone.*

The overstated hatred for the Dutch gives the poem unity and focus. This elegy, though obviously a youthful effort, is witty and sophisticated in its elaborate argument; but the exuberant praise of Vere — calling him metaphorically England's *Primum Mobile,* tutelar god, and Prometheus — strains the reader's credibility and dilutes the effect of the poem. The excesses of wit, complexity, and metaphor make Felltham's "Elegie on Henry Earl of Oxford" more of an interesting and virtuoso exercise-piece than a successful elegy.

Coming from the pen of one who twenty-one years later was to call the executed Charles I "Christ the Second," Felltham's "On the Duke of Buckingham slain by Felton, the 23. Aug. 1628" is a remarkably cool and objective occasional poem. Buckingham, Charles's chief minister, badly bungled England's wars against Spain and France. Parliament threatened impeachment proceedings against him in June 1628, and probably would have carried them out had not the King dissolved that group. When a naval lieutenant two months later stabbed Buckingham to death at Portsmouth, the duke's assassination had both political and religious overtones. The King's Puritan antagonists saw the death as a blow against both political tyranny and what they considered the pro-Papal leanings of the Establishment. And even thoughtful members of Charles's government were relieved — though they did not admit it openly — that the impetuous minister was no longer there to force them into disaster. Felltham, a loyal supporter of Crown and Established Church, both admired and distrusted the duke; and, though he was startled by the assassination, he understood the joy with which it was greeted by Buckingham's many and diverse enemies. This complexity of thought and feeling, held in almost total suspension, gives Felltham's occasional poem a tension seldom found outside the lyric.

Felltham marvels at the inglorious way in which this great man died:

> Can a knife
> Let out so many Titles and a life?

> Now I'le mourn thee! Oh that so huge a pile
> Of State should pash thus in so small a while!

For all the apparent greatness of the much honored Buckingham, he
has fallen to a knife. Felltham is aware of the rejoicing of those
Puritans and others in Parliament who feared that Buckingham was
helping to lead England back to Rome: "Let the rude *Genius* of the
giddy Train,/Brag in a fury that they have stabb'd *Spain,/Austria,*
and the skipping *French. . . .*" Synthesizing the extremes of
Buckingham's position of greatness and the great hatred which his
detractors felt toward him and which has led to his fall, Felltham ex-
claims:

> Thou art to me
> The great Example of Mortality.
> And when the times to come shall want a Name
> To startle Greatnesse, here is BUCKINGHAM
> Faln like a Meteor. . . .

Felltham, then, sees the death of Buckingham in terms very similar
to the medieval concept of tragedy: the fall of a high-placed individual. Having presented in general terms the position of
Buckingham's enemies, Felltham turns to the actual assassin, John
Felton:

> 'tis hard to say
> Whether it was that went the stranger way,
> Thou [Buckingham] or the hand that slew thee: thy Estate
> Was high, and he was resolute above that.

Refusing to discuss Buckingham's character (" 'Tis undue/ To speak
ill of the Dead though it be true"), Felltham acknowledges the slain
Duke's former position of eminence:

> even those that envy'd thee confesse,
> Thou hadst a Mind, a flowing Noblenesse,
> A Fortune, Friends, and such proportion,
> As call for sorrow, to be thus undone.

Throughout, Felltham opposes Buckingham's greatness with his
enemies' hatred for him and the duke's estate with his assassin's
resolution. Finding in Buckingham a "great Example of Mortality,"

Felltham sorrows at his fall not because the duke was a worthy man but because his fall was unworthy of his position. Fearing the extremism that can result in the fall of "so huge a pile/ Of State" as Buckingham, Felltham pleads for moderation. Assuming the position of those who rejoice at the fall of the duke, Felltham can almost be convinced of the rightness of Felton's deed:

> Yet should I speake the Vulgar, I should boast
> Thy bold Assassinate, and wish almost
> He were no Christian, that I up might stand,
> To praise th'intent of his mis-guided hand.
> And sure when all the Patriots in the shade
> Shall rank, and their full musters there be made,
> He shall sit next to *Brutus*, and receive
> Such Bayes as Heath'nish ignorance can give.

But, to Felltham, doing evil to reach good ends is not the Christian way; hence the assassin cannot be considered a patriot. Since Felton is a Christian, there is nothing admirable about his bold deed. Even the most rabid opponents of Buckingham should realize that, "Though he did good, he did it the wrong way." By using the common bonds of Christianity as the pivot in his argument, Felltham suggests a way to bring together the opposing groups. Both are Christian, and both must surely see that for a nation to survive there must be rule of law: "They oft decine into the worst of ill,/That act the Peoples wish without Laws will."

This poem about the death of Buckingham is not an elegy, for Felltham uses the death of the spectacularly successful and passionately hated Buckingham to plead for moderation and the rule of law and to expose the power and danger of fanaticism. He concludes his poem, however, not by ranting against extremists, but by indicating the reconciliation implicit in the bonds of Christianity common to all Englishmen. The twenty-five-year-old Felltham is a thoughtful observer of the political situation, and his poem is no less than remarkable. The carefully structured tension between the great heights which Buckingham attained and the great hatred in which he was held, along with the powerful language of the poem, make these verses about Buckingham one of Felltham's most effective pieces.

In 1628, Felltham dedicated the Long Century of *Resolves* to Thomas, Lord Coventry. The young essayist was not at that time acquainted with the Lord Keeper of the Great Seal, but he knew him

by reputation, as the first sentence of the Epistle Dedicatory indicates: "Though I should not know your *Person*, I cannot bee a
stranger to your *Vertues*." Lord Coventry was almost unique among
Charles I's courtiers in that his honesty was admitted by everyone —
even by the Puritans who despised the bench at which he sat, the
prerogative court of Star Chamber. When Coventry died in 1640,
after fifteen years of service as Lord Keeper, Felltham composed a
tribute to him, "On Thomas Lord Coventry, Lord Keeper of the
Great Seal."

The poem, although long, has little to distinguish it. Coventry is
praised for his honesty, a trait all too rare in the judges of the day:
"Who can dispatch so much so well, so free/From Fear, from
Favour, stain or Bribery?" There may have been more brilliant
justices than Coventry, but, Felltham boasts, neither

> *More*'s learned wit,
> Nor *Bacon*'s miracl'd Fancy e're can sit
> Loftier in Fames high Tower, than what we see
> Flows from his lasting Names integrity.

Moreover, Coventry's sittings were models of what such should be:
"His were not Courts alone, but Readings; there/The Bar was
throng'd rather to learn than hear."

By far the most interesting element of the poem, however, is
Felltham's ingenious application of the elegiac convention that has
all nature weeping for the deceased:

> 'Tis not an Angle, Province, that or this
> That weeps: The general Kingdom Mourner is.
> Nor is't a Plank or prop that's lost by Fate,
> But 'tis a Capital Column of the State.
> Which here so summons grief, that all men good
> Approach, and bring sad Tribute to the floud:
> That now this Isle not onely seems to be
> Inviron'd round with waves, but waves to be.
> Our *London* is turn'd *Venice*, and our gay
> Pallaces peer, as plac'd in a salt Bay.
> Where Tydes of sorrow make us think we meet
> Not men on Land, but Rowers in the street.

The poem's lack of excitement and sparkle is probably a result of its
subject's lack of those qualities. Coventry did his job competently;

but while he was a solid and honest man, he was also unexciting and unassuming. He had no dramatic reversals in his career, and he died peacefully. Felltham undoubtedly did as much as he could with the materials available to him.

In 1643, the Puritan dominated Parliament sat and passed legislation about Christmas Day that abolished by implication the celebration of what the Puritans considered a pagan festival. Felltham's reaction is expressed in the poem "Upon Abolishing the Feast of the Nativity of our blessed Saviour." Felltham opens his protest by asking why, if "each petty Princes Birth" is celebrated, "the Lord of Life's blest day/Be thrown away?" In the second stanza, he opposes the fundamentalist argument that, since the exact date of Christ's birth is unknown, it is blasphemous to set arbitrarily a day for celebration of the event. To Felltham, "just power" commands him to set aside one day each year to commemorate the Birth; and December 25 "as well shall stand" as any. Felltham climaxes his poem by stating an argument completely abhorrent to the Puritans: since God, as king, has not expressly forbidden such a commemoration and since the Church, as viceroy of God on earth, has through tradition set a specific date, he will continue the celebration of Yule and "Will Christian dye."

The poem, written in a ten-line stanza of mixed iambic tetrameter and dimeter, is not among Felltham's better efforts. It achieved, however, some attention among the Puritans; one of them published a broadside in which he set forth Felltham's poem and answered it with a similarly constructed one of his own.[19] The thrust of this anonymous Puritan's argument is that God would have revealed the exact day of the Nativity "had he thought fit it should/Be kept as now some People would." Moreover, to give the Church the arbitrary power of fixing the day of Christmas can lead straight to Rome:

> If one, why not six, ten or more?
> Or why not as well Fifteen Score
> As Papists have almost already
> Dedicat to their Saints and Lady?

The ultimate argument against ecclesiastical tradition is, of course, the fundamentalist one: "To be no more than's Written wise/Shall me Suffice." Unfortunately, both Felltham's poem and the Puritan poet's "full Refutation" of Felltham's argument now possess a

merely historical interest, but a comparison of the two clearly shows
Felltham's distinct superiority in the use of language.

By far the most controversial religious figure in the court of
Charles I was William Laud, who was made Archbishop of Canterbury in 1633. From the beginning of his ecclesiastical career, Laud
antagonized the English Puritans by his insistence on uniformity and
ritualism in the Church; and he infuriated the Scottish Kirk by urg-
ing the King to impose upon it a Prayer Book which would have led
the Scots into Anglicanism. The Puritan controlled Long Parliament
arrested Laud in 1640 and tried him for treason. Finding insufficient
evidence to execute him through normal judicial channels, that body
condemned him by legislative means in an act of attainder. Felltham
marked Laud's execution and set forth his own attitude toward the
Archbishop in a thirty-line Latin epitaph, "In *Gulielmi Laud.*"

Enjoining "Stupensce Viator! et Miranda Fati lege" (Traveler,
learn of a fantastic calamity and stand amazed!), Felltham rehearses
many points of the Archbishop's life: his lowly birth, his trouble with
the Scots, his four-year imprisonment, his trial before Parliament,
the extralegal fashion in which he was condemned, and the dignity
with which he met his death. In Laud's execution, Parliament has, in
Felltham's opinion, condemned England to a period of virtual
chaos:

> Quocum Majestas Principum, Procerum Tutela,
> Ecclesiæ Patrimonium,
> Libertas Subjecti,
> Et Britannici orbis immunitas,
> Simul pro tempore Tumulantur.

(With him, the grandeur of the Kingdom, the defence of the Cavaliers,/The
tradition of the Church,/The freedom of the subjects,/And the safety of the
British sphere/Are, for a season, buried together.)

This poem is of considerable historical and biographical interest; and
its formal and measured statement of personal outrage and grief exhibits Felltham's considerable skill in Latin composition.

The poem that Felltham's nineteenth-century admirers found
most difficult to excuse is "An Epitaph to the Eternal Memory of
Charles the First, King of Great Britain, France and Ireland, &c.
Inhumanely murthered by a perfidious Party of His prevalent Subjects, Jan. 30, 1648." Despite Felltham's excess of zeal — what some
have considered blasphemy in the last line — the poem is a highly
successful exercise in rhetoric; it sweeps the reader along until he ex-

pects, and would be somehow disappointed without, the outrage of its climax. The epitaph is tightly constructed, and it consists entirely of clauses introduced by the adverb "when," a word which in itself builds anticipation.

Beginning with only the exaggerations that one would expect from an impassioned supporter of the monarchy, Felltham argues Charles's right and ability to rule:

> When He had shewn the world, that He was King
> Of all those Vertues that can Honour bring;
> And by His Princely Graces made it known,
> That Rule was so inherently His Own,
> That His great Parts might justly Him prefer
> Not to two Isles, but the worlds Emperor.
> When His large Soul in sufferings had out-shin'd
> All *Jobs* vast Patience: and in His clear Mind
> Had rivall'd *Solomons* Wisdom, but out-gone
> His Temperance, in His most tempting Throne.

When Felltham joins to Charles's position as sovereign of the state his role as Supreme Governor of the Church, he still exaggerates Charles's abilities, but perhaps no more than might be expected from the author of *Resolves:*

> When by a Noble Christian Fortitude,
> He had serenely tryumph'd o're all rude
> And barbarous Indignities that men
> (Inspir'd from Hell) could act by hand or pen.
> When He to save the Church had shed His blood,
> And dy'd for being (onely) Wise and Good:
> When His three Kingdoms in a well-weigh'd sense
> He'd rather lose, than a good Conscience:
> As knowing, 'twas a far more glorious thing
> To dye a MARTYR, than to live a KING.

In the next few clauses, the poet begins to go beyond even the excess of praise allowed in a seventeenth-century commendatory poem, but the reader who has stayed with Felltham this far will hesitate to lay the poem aside as incredible; he is now enthralled by the power of the language and by the sweep of the emotion:

> When He had copy'd out in every Line,
> Our Saviours Passion (bating the Divine)
> Nay, even His Prayers and Gospel, if we look

> Impartially upon his peerlesse Book;
> A Book so rarely good, we read in one
> The Psalms and Proverbs, *David-Solomon;*
> With all that high-born Charity, which shines
> Quite through the great Apostles sacred lines:
> That, spight of rage, next future Ages shall
> Hold it (with Reverence stamp'd) Canonical.

There is left for the poet in such a situation only one possible direction in which to advance his subject any further — higher than canonization of his book, there is canonization of the man himself, and after that the ultimate:

> When *Herod, Judas, Pilate,* and the *Jews,*
> *Scots, Cromwell, Bradshaw,* and the shag-haird *Mews*
> Had quite out-acted, and by their damn'd Cry
> Of injur'd Justice, lessened Crucifie:
> When He had prov'd, that since the world began,
> So many Tears were never shed for Man:
> Since so belov'd he fell, that with pure grief
> His Subjects dy'd, 'cause he was reft of Life:
> When to convince the Heretick worlds base thought,
> His Royal Bloud true miracles had wrought:
> When it appear'd, He to this world was sent,
> The Glory of KINGS, but Shame of PARLIAMENT:
> The stain of th'*English,* that can never dye;
> The Protestants perpetual Infamy:
> When He had rose thus, Truths great Sacrifice,
> *Here CHARLES the First, and CHRIST the second lyes.*

The poem progresses, then, from divine right to divinity.

Impartial historians, more knowledgeable about the machinations of Charles's government than Felltham and having a broader perspective than the poet, disagree almost totally with Felltham's view of that unfortunate monarch's wisdom, abilities, and motivations. They even dispute Charles's authorship of that "peerlesse Book" *Eikon Basilike,* which the King supposedly wrote while awaiting execution. But such matters are irrelevant in a discussion of the poem's merit, because Felltham is writing not so much about the historical Charles as he is about the ideal Charles. A king should be divinely called to his throne; he should be wise, patient, and just; he should promote unity in state and Church; he should oppose a factious and extreme Parliament; he should devote his last days to the composition of a devotional book. The martyred monarch of Felltham's poem is all that a king ideally should be, and in this context his deification is less outrageous than it is just.

Taken in its historical context, Felltham's comments on Charles are no more excessive than are many of the statements made by the Parliamentarian side. The poem is an exaggeration, certainly, but it is overstatement in the direction of idealism. In it is a real feeling of outrage and righteous indignation, and the tone is a rich mixture of bitterness and Stoic trustfulness in a final retribution. Felltham's greatest achievement in the poem, however, is the careful progression of metaphors building subtly and inevitably toward its conclusion; this epitaph on Charles is a moving poem precisely because of the masterful rhetoric that everywhere controls its statement.

Felltham's poems on religious and political topics are not — with the exception of the poems about Buckingham and about Charles — among his best occasional verse. The complexity of attitude found in the Buckingham poem and the impassioned, yet controlled statement of the epitaph for the executed king make these two poems among the most significant of Felltham's literary works.

III *Miscellaneous Occasional Poems*

Felltham's remaining occasional poems are about a variety of subjects and persons, and they are of several types: reflective, elegiac, commendatory, and satiric. The two reflective poems bear on subjects treated in prose in *Resolves*. "True Happinesse" describes Christian contentment and lists the ingredients necessary to it. Man can find true happiness only in the *via media:*

> If 'bove the mean his mind be pitcht,
> Or with unruly Passions twicht,
> A storm is there: But he sails most
> Secure, whose Bark in any Coast
> Can neither be becalm'd nor tost.

Man can be truly content when he has "A chearful, but an upright heart," the result of God's having bestowed on him "a clear and temperate spirit." As for more material matters, Felltham admits that a man should have

> Wealth to keep want away, and Fear
> Of it: Not More: some Friends, still near,

> And chosen well: nor must he misse
> A Calling: yet, some such as is
> Imployment; not a Businesse.

Moderation is the key, along with caution; and the statement about man's employment is an echo of Felltham's favorite Old Testament book, Ecclesiastes, wherein man is urged to find the kind of work that he likes to do in order that labor will not be a burden to him.

Finally, in matters of a more devotional nature, Felltham warns that to be content man's "soul must hug no private sin," and that "God built he must be in his mind;/That is, part God: whose faith no wind/Can shake." But, above all, man should develop in himself a Stoic acceptance of the vicissitudes of human existence: "Life as a middle way, immur'd/With Joy and Grief, to be indur'd,/Not spurn'd, nor wanton'd hence. . . ."

"True Happinesse" fails to realize much of its potential because of faulty versification and an essentially prosaic subject. In this instance, Felltham does not handle the short line effectively; the entirely too frequent run-on lines and the often consequent full stops in the middle of lines create a choppy effect. Moreover, the poem lacks the fresh and powerful imagery characteristic of Felltham's best poetry.

In "Considerations of one design'd for a Nunnery," Felltham presents arguments for and against monastic life. The first argument against that kind of existence is a typically Protestant one; a life of contemplation and of prayer for the repose of the dead is not efficacious:

> What can my being thus a cold Recluse
> Be to th'advantage of my Parents souls?
> My Charity shall be my own, not theirs;
> Nor can my Vigils or abstemious frost,
> Or cool or expiate, the smallest fume
> Of their intemperate heat. . . .

Furthermore, if chastity were the proper conduct in life and if his parents had followed that path, then, the speaker declares, "I had/No being had at all. . . ."

There are, of course, benefits to be derived by entering a nunnery, but Felltham regards those who do so as escaping the duties and worries of life:

> To avoid the thraldom of imperious Love,
> The hazards of contempt, and calumny,
> The heats and Hecticks both of Fear, and Love,
> The qualms, and throws of Married life, the frets
> And cumbers, humming 'bout the Heards of families:
> To ride secure out of the reach of Fortune,
> O're-looking all those rouling tides of Fate,
> Which worldlings still are hurried with; and then
> To be wrapt up in Innocence, a Privado
> Dear, and familiar to the Deity,
> Is surely a condition to be catcht at,
> With all th'expansions both of mind, and body.

Such resignation from the world is unnatural, however:

> But then again to weigh the Cancelling
> Of what I'm born to, tugging all my life
> Against the Tyde; still streining up the hill:
> The Plains and pleasant Vallies ever hidden.
> What is it lesse then the bold undertaking
> Of perpetual war with Nature?

Reflecting the same sentiments expressed in *Resolves* L. 85, "Of Marriage, and single life," the speaker of the poem asks:

> does not Nature in her general course,
> Design all Creatures to their fixed end?
> Did the wise God of Nature give me Sex
> Onely to cast it off? were all our flames
> Rais'd, to be kept but in perpetual smother?

And then the speaker answers:

> Our Passions, our Affections and Desires,
> We are injoyn'd to regulate, not deposite quite.
> Why were their Objects lent us, set before
> Our open eyes, and we forbid to view them?
> Our joyes, our hopes, the feathers of the soul,
> Were never meant us to become our torment.

The poem climaxes with a consideration of the dual nature of man's existence:

> If Love be fire,
> As 'tis the blaze of life, it then must have
> Fuel to feed on. All spiritual is
> Too fine for flesh to live by; and too grosse
> Is food corporeal all: As man is mixt,
> So his affections object must.

Having accepted this notion, the speaker declares that "Love temper'd right/Is chaste as cold Virginity," and he vows to live as "my wise Creator did appoint me" and not to "Lock up in forced chains my free-born Soul."

Although the outcome of the reflection mirrored in "Considerations of one design'd for a Nunnery" is almost a foregone conclusion and although Felltham may be unfair in his presentation of the benefits of monastic life, the piece is nevertheless a fine one. The deft control of its blank verse, frequently and purposefully irregular, gives it a conversational tone and a sincerity that is appropriate to its subject matter. Its striking images and lines ("abstemious frost," "a condition to be catcht at," "perpetual smother," "the feathers of the soul") move it far away from the prosaic nature of "True Happinesse."

Felltham's considerable skill and power as an elegist has already been noted in the discussions of his poems occasioned by the deaths of important literary, religious, and political figures. Felltham did not, however, confine his elegiac writings to subjects of wide public concern; he wrote many poems — brief epitaphs and longer elegies — about the deaths of persons little known then and completely unknown to the modern reader. Such occasional poems as these must stand entirely on their poetic merits if they stand at all, and it is remarkable how often Felltham succeeds in evoking an emotional response from the reader to the passing of virtually anonymous individuals.

Some of his epitaphs attempt little and consequently achieve little. "An Epitaph on Robert Lord Spencer" is a brief exercise in praise of a Northamptonshire neighbor. "Upon My Father's Tomb" is of interest primarily for its biographical materials and its shape — on both the marble tomb and the printed page of *Lusoria*, the words of this Latin epitaph form a sepulchral urn. However, neither Felltham's attempt to write a shaped poem nor the shape of this particular epitaph is unusual. Many poets of the earlier seventeenth century — most notably George Herbert — wrote shaped verse, and one of the most common shapes attempted in funereal verse was the urn. "An Epitaph on the Lady Mary Farmor," written in praise of the mother of Felltham's employer and patroness, the Countess of Thomond, is of interest for its use of the term "strong Line" and for its concluding simple but wholly satisfying statement: "Here lies the best Example of her Sex."

Four of Felltham's brief epitaphs are particularly striking in both statement and imagery. The first four lines of "On a hopeful Youth" call to mind Ben Jonson's best efforts in the genre:

> Stay Passenger, and lend a tear,
> Youth and Vertue both lye here.
> Reading this know thou hast seen
> Vertue tomb'd at but Fifteen.

The fourth line of Felltham's tribute to this anonymous adolescent is as moving in its classic simplicity as "here doth lye/*Ben. Jonson* his best piece of *poetrie*" and "Under-neath this stone doth lye/As much beautie as could dye."

At the other extreme, "On the Lady *E. M.*" is striking in its witty central metaphor:

> Her Prudence, Wit and Memory being told,
> Death seiz'd her streight; mistook her to be old.
> A sheet of *Bacon's* catch'd at more, we know,
> Than all sad *Fox*, long *Holinshead* or *Stow*.
> She was but Eight; yet judgment had such store,
> Upon a just Compute she dy'd Threescore.
> Ladies, take heed how to be wise you try,
> For 'tis resolv'd, who will be wise must dye.

The pithy, aphoristic quality of the lines is as effective as that in the other brief epitaphs examined. The poem is quite clever, of course, but the witty comparison of the length of human life to that of various prose writings is completely appropriate in its context. Moreover, the wit is balanced effectively by the sad tenderness of the last line, with its strong sense of Stoicism and its wistful allusion to Felltham's own lifelong literary project.

Somewhat longer and more ambitious are "On Mr. Mynshull" and "Epitaph on Sir *John Done*, Kt." In the former, Felltham describes two periods in the life of a virtuous man. His youth was peerless:

> Imagine Man unfaln! constant to Truth:
> Thereby you may collect what was his Youth.
> Propose the Schools in practice, marry the Arts
> To sweetnesse, till they prove a charm for hearts:
> Erect a Centre, where the fervent Love
> Of Lord and Labourer together move
> And meet: till there be made by it agen
> Atonement 'twixt the worlds frail gods and men.

And in his maturity Mynshull represented "Th' unfound *Idea* of a perfect friend." In both cases, the statements, though exaggerations, are felicitously presented in beautiful imagery drawn from Neoplatonic philosophy.

In "Epitaph on Sir *John Done*, Kt.," Felltham makes quite effective use of the Phoenix myth in conjecturing what would have happened had Done been cremated:

> But as the *Arabian* bird th' doth consume
> Herself is renovated by perfume,
> So he had lives refin'd and by the spice
> Of his own vertues prov'd a wonder twice
> To light the world, and man. . . .

The fiery metaphor then expands into the final conflagration:

> When the great Blaze shall clasp the universe,
> . . . .
> So much his spirit doth his flesh control
> That one spark shall flash it to his soul.

So good has been the life of this man that there will be no trouble rejoining his body to his soul when that becomes necessary for the Last Judgment.

Felltham also wrote elegies about the deaths of people now little remembered. "An Elegie on the honorable and Excellent Mistress M. Coventry" commemorates the Lord Keeper's daughter-in-law and contains two memorable passages. In the first one, this modest woman — naturally beautiful because pure of soul — is contrasted to those members of her sex who use cosmetics in a vain attempt to appear beautiful:

> Beauty and feature both since she is gone,
> Suffer Eclipse and Diminution.

> And this is it, which makes most ladies known,
> Borrow from Art, what now is not their own,
> That in the face, where harmless Ignorance
> Thinks beauty sits, lies *Italy* and *France*.

In the second memorable passage, Mary Coventry's chastity is seen as "Virgin Ice rob'd with a Maiden Snow"; yet she was no nun. She lived in the world, but she was untouched by its evil:

> The Industrious Bee, that midst her Honey lives
> Yet un-intangled keeps her wing, and thrives
> In her own stock of sweetness, told how she
> Liv'd in the World, from the World's mazes free.

Jean Robertson, viewing this passage as reflecting "the neo-platonic conception of the soul as a prisoner in the body," is misleading in her assertion that this concept, "a continually recurring image in the *Resolves*, makes one of its less frequent appearances in the Poems."[20] In many of Felltham's poems, most notably his love lyrics, Neoplatonism occurs as a thematic, as well as a dramatic, element.

Felltham's "Elegie on Mr. *Fra. Leigh*, who dyed of the Plague, May-day, 1637," shows some of the poet's best, and unfortunately some of his less attractive, habits of mind. With aristocratic paternalism, Felltham contrasts the deaths of the poor to the death of a gentleman:

> the Plague which humbly fed,
> And onely th'unfann'd Vulgar harrassed;
> Perhaps in pity, for to them a Grave
> Is far more blest than that poor life they have;
> Now is exalted grown, and shews more grim,
> Boding a stroke at Gentry thorough him. . . .

In his beautiful and lavish praise of Leigh, an otherwise unknown young lawyer or law student, Felltham shows his ability for apt expression; and he displays a poet's knowledge of just how much to undercut that praise to make it credible:

> Hopeful *Leigh* is dead!
> Dead of the Plague! dead in his early Youth!
> Leaving quite widowed Handsomnesse and Truth.
> His shape was womans envy, and her stain;
> His mind all sweet, his Conversation gain

> To all, to whom he did the honour grant
> T' enjoy those parts, which Nobles boast, yet want.
> If he had errors, they were such as ne'r
> Could grow to faults, but the next riper year
> Would clean have chac'd away. For as from fire
> At the first kindling some smoak will aspire;
> So youth must be allow'd his vapours, which
> Maturity and time will turn to rich
> And brightning flames. . . .

Felltham laments the passing of a scholar and patron of letters in "On Sir Rowland Cotton, famous for Letters and other Parts." Cotton's knowledge of languages is treated in a sparkling metaphor:

> sure he knew
> More Tongues than were at *Babels* building new:
> And in so many Languages could write,
> That he's learn'd now, that can but name them right.

Many of the poem's images are, appropriately, drawn from printing: Cotton was Nature's "Index"; his virtuous death was a "fair concordance" to his virtuous life; and while he lived he was able to distinguish well between true and false knowledge:

> That *Rubrick* Sea of Learning which do's drown
> *Niles* rash Impostors with their puft-up Crown,
> Fled before him checking her waves, and there
> To his sharp judgment left her bottom bare.

Other biographical details are given in similarly apt metaphors. Cotton, once an outstanding athlete, was during much of his mature life a cripple. In heraldic terms, Felltham equates him with that fabulous bird which had no feet and which was consequently fated to lifelong flight:

> Thus the not using feet of so rich price,
> Shew'd how he grew a bird of Paradise,
> Scorning the flag of man, till he became
> Volant above in a Celestial flame. . . .

Felltham's tribute to this scholar who "did converse/Not with some Nations, but the Universe" is truly a virtuoso performance.

Felltham wrote five commendatory poems. All — in both subject matter and imagery — are very much the products of their age. The brief poem "Upon a rare Voice" compares a singer's performance to that of "some bright star in the supremest Round"; such allusions to the music of the spheres are ubiquitous in Renaissance literature. The poem, hardly more than a six-line exercise, is beautiful even if it is a bit pretentious and highly derivative.

The commendatory poem of Felltham's that may seem most grotesque to the modern reader, though poems on similar subjects are quite common in the seventeenth century, is "On a Gentlewoman, whose Nose was pitted with the Small Pox." When the poet asks why the disease should leave its traces on "The graceful Promont of her face" rather than on her cheek or eye, he answers that this enemy of beauty could not overthrow the "Rose and Snow" of the one or combat successfully the "look and shine" of the other. He then makes a virtue of the disfigurement. Speaking to the disease, he asserts:

> thou too feeble to controul
> The Guest within, her purer soul,
> Hast out of spleen to things of grace,
> Left thy sunk footsteps in the place.

And comforting the woman, the speaker concludes: "Face-scars do not disgrace, but shew/Valour well freed from a bold foe." The poem, with such circuitous and paradoxical logic, is very much of its time; it is reminiscent of John Dryden's first published poem, "Upon the Death of Lord Hastings" (1649), in which smallpox blisters contain tears that are shed for the victim.

Probably the most conventional of this group of Felltham's commendatory poems is one that celebrates a popular athletic event and its sponsor, "To Mr. *Dover* on his Cotswold Games." Despite the poem's announced subjects, Felltham seems more concerned with the Muses and Mount Helicon than with athletic competitions and Mount Olympus. Seeing this revival of the "Olimpick" games as fulfillment of the "feign'd stories" of "old Poets," he prophesies for Dover: "future times will learn to title thee/That *Youth'd Apollo*." The poem is well-unified and is often striking in its wit, but it suffers — as do most poems written for such occasions — in being somewhat mechanical and contrived.

Four of Felltham's poems, two commendatory and two satirical, serve as a transition into a consideration of his love lyrics. Before discussing these four poems, there needs to be a brief review of one of the conventions available to Felltham in the writing of amorous verse.[21] Most of the love poetry written during the Renaissance was in one way or another affected by the attitudes expressed toward love by Francesco Petrarch and by the rich tradition founded on his *Canzoniere*. In the Petrarchan pattern, the lady who is the subject of the verses is beautiful, causing the poet to desire her greatly. She is, however, also morally pure; and she is usually of a higher social station than he. Because she is both pure and noble, she scorns his suit. The poet usually occupies himself in composing detailed, and often extravagant, descriptions of his lady's physical beauty; in commenting on her purity of soul; in exulting in the merest glimpse of her; and in writhing under her scorn. His existence vacillates between excesses of joy and excesses of gloom. Yet always the lady is worshipped and the poet debased. Some English erotic poems of the Renaissance betray complete acceptance of the Petrarchan tradition; but others — especially many of those written near the end of the sixteenth century and during the earlier seventeenth century — consciously reject the convention.

While neither Felltham's "To the Painter taking the Picture of the Lady *Penelope* Countesse of Peterburgh" nor his "To the Lady *D. S.*" is a love poem, both reflect the Petrarchan love tradition. Penelope O'Brien Mordaunt (died 1702) was the daughter of Barnabas and Mary, Earl and Countess of Thomond, and the wife of Henry, Earl of Peterborough. A famous beauty in her young womanhood, she is mentioned favorably more than once by that admirer of beautiful women Samuel Pepys.[22] Employing a genre that Andrew Marvell was later to use quite effectively in satire, the instructions-to-a-painter poem, Felltham praises and flatters the daughter of his patroness; but he warns the artist not to draw a good likeness:

> Forbear! This face, if taken true,
> Ruines thine Art: For when men view
> So new a model of a Face,
> So chaste, so sweet, 'twill quite disgrace
> All thy old Rules. . . .

He catalogs the lady's facial features, employing the *blason* device found everywhere in poems of the Petrarchan tradition:

> For either Cheek, when you begin,
> Draw me a smiling Cherubin.
> For lips thou maist the *Gemini* track
> Of some high Holy-day *Zodiack*:
> For Brow and eyes thou shalt display
> The Ev'n and Morn, Creations day. . . .

And he concludes by advising the painter to place himself in the position of a worshipper:

> Last, draw thy self and Pencil thrown
> Beneath her feet: For 'twill be known
> She's mistresse of far braver Arts,
> Thou Faces tak'st, but she takes Hearts.

Even though the subject of the poem is not a lady whom the poet loves, these verses are written entirely within the Petrarchan convention. In the descriptive catalog, however, Felltham substitutes religious metaphors for the traditional ones drawn from nature and the classics; and he thereby imparts to otherwise conventional lines some small measure of personality.

"To the Lady *D. S.*" is a more complex and more interesting picture of a woman's beauty. Perhaps taking a hint from John Donne, who was fond of using scientific and mathematical metaphors in unusual contexts, Felltham praises the lady in Euclidian terms:

> He must write measure, that would write of You.
> So Geometrical has Nature fram'd
> That, which can now no otherwise be nam'd,
> But as a Rule for all: each several part
> Is all whole Axiome, to direct an Art.
> That now, men skilful, doubt, to which is due,
> More to those noble Sciences, or You.

In a more traditional, Petrarchan description of the lady, he asks who can be unmoved,

>   while your eye
> Kindles each noble bloud with such chaste fire,
> As causes Flame, and yet forbids Desire?
> And when your skye of vein shall gently flow
> Branching through both your Hemispheres of snow,
> When crimson Tulips, and the Rose o'th'bush,

> Shall draw their tincture from your lip, and blush;
> When that mild breath, which even the calmest West
> Fannes from the Pink and Violet, from your brest
> Shall have its derivation; then you may
> Confesse your self, our Morning and our Day.

Although this lush physical perfection will inevitably fade, the lady's reputation shall never dim since her inward beauty matches her outward perfection:

> that pure shine of Deity, your Mind,
> So fill'd with sweetnesse, that whosoe're shall see't,
> Streight thinks of Virgin Nature, at whose feet
> Stand all the Sects of old Philosophy,
> Paying their admiration by their eye.
> So you amaze all knowledge, that even they
> Which can but name and know you, do adde day
> Unto their owne Life here.

References to philosophy and knowledge recall the sciences spoken of near the beginning of the poem and neatly but unobtrusively give a circular unity to the poem. In these commendatory lines, Felltham merges learned, intellectual metaphors with romantic, conventional ones — a technique employed in some of his best love lyrics.

The final two poems to be considered in this section are playful satires on the relationship between the sexes. Sometime in the earlier seventeenth century, an unknown woman, clearly tired of the numerous complaints of male poets about their unsuccessful love affairs, wrote a six-line poem in which she warns: "Believe not him whom Love hath left so wise,/As to have power his own tale to tell;/ . . . . /In well-told Love most often falshood lyes."[23] Felltham's "Answer" denies the woman's thesis, for he alleges that love "can make Ideots wise" and that it "tips the tongue as well as wounds the heart." One who loves and loses silently "Hath heart and passion weak"; strong passion "Can make the dumb to speak." The answer, while lively and clever in its statement, is merely an exercise, a trivial piece of Petrarchan complaint.

"Gunemastix" (that is, The Female Scourge), the longest poem in Felltham's canon, consists of seventy-eight heroic couplets. The first 138 lines are the ultimate comment in the "cruel fair" convention of the Petrarchan tradition. Women, through their beauty, cause men to love them, but the love objects then scorn that love. Probably basing his remarks on Juvenal's sixth satire, Felltham lists everything that he can find wrong about women:

> Commend a Womans mercy? 'Tis to say
> Tygers are kind, to mis-call night for day.
>
> . . . .
>
>   Nature turning Tyrant, woman made
> Mens spirits scourge; instructing her to trade
> In racking of their souls, to flame their hearts,
> And to dissect them in a thousand parts.
>   Their looks indeed speak pity, but they are
> Like Fowlers shraps, pleasing but to insnare;
>
> . . . .
>
> Live among women! ah, thou more safely maist
> Sleep in a bed with Snakes, with Scorpions jest:
>
> . . . .
>
> She's mischiefs powder-plot! that at one blow
> Gave Man and all the world an Overthrow.
>
> . . . .
>
> The Serpent sure that tempted her could be
> But a meer Type of one more subtle, she
>
> . . . .
>
> Oh you Celestial Powers! why did you lend
> Accursed man a soul, to be impenn'd
> In womens breasts; who use it with despite . . . ?

Then after this tirade, the speaker abruptly admits that "Passion and Fury pulls that from my pen/I never thought of. . . ." And without warning, he praises those members of the fair sex who do not disdain men:

>   they are to men
>   (When they are loving) things so precious,

> That man out of their sight is ruinous
> Whatever large Philosophy could find
> Of Vertue, had *Idea* from their mind.

. . . .

> And I have heard, when Heaven and Nature did
> Study what blessings to put on mans head,
> It was agreed (his ruines to repair)
> He should enjoy a Woman good, kind, fair.

The poem, though excessively long, is often witty and possesses an attractive playfulness. The sudden reversal at the end may be too easy a device to be successful, but Donald Cornu's claim that "Gunemastix" shows that Felltham "was not temperamentally fitted for satire" is perhaps too strong.[24]

   These miscellaneous poems vary greatly in their worth, ranging from the trivial "Upon a rare Voice" to the impressive "To the Lady *D. S.*" to the beautiful and lyrical elegies and brief epitaphs. They also, of course, deal with extremely diverse subject matter and reveal Felltham in a variety of moods and stances. The poems which utilize Petrarchan conventions are particularly interesting in that they serve as a bridge between Felltham's occasional and erotic poetry.

IV   *Love Lyrics*

Of the sixteen love lyrics in Felltham's *Lusoria*, some are ingenious exercises written to an imaginary, scornful young lady; others are moving and personal statements. The simplest and least personal of Felltham's lyrics are in the Petrarchan tradition, but the more complex and emotionally moving poems reflect the influence of John Donne and the Metaphysicals as well as that of Jonson and the Cavaliers. Taken as a whole, Felltham's small group of love poems exemplifies the most important characteristics of seventeenth-century secular poetry.

   The most earnestly Petrarchan of Felltham's poems is "The Amazement," in which the beauty of the speaker's mistress is effectively cataloged in conventional Petrarchan terms:

> See the Roses being blown,
>   Shed their leaves and fall alone,
> As shamed by a purer red of hers.
>   See the Clowds that cast their snow,

Which melts as soon as 'tis below,
When but a whiter white of her appears.
See the Silk-worme how she weaves
Her self to death among her leaves,
As broke with envy of her finer hairs.

In "The Sun and Wind," the young lady is typically scornful of the would-be lover. The sun of the title represents her beauty; the wind, her "coy disdain." The final stanza, though conventional, presents an interesting paradox:

So though thy Sun heats my desire,
Yet know thy coy disdain
Falls like a storm on that young fire,
So blowes me cool again.

Another poem, "The Appeal," begs Cupid to set the lover free since the "Tyrant" boy has caused him to "love a rock." "On a Jewel given at parting" employs the same image; the lover, having given his "freshly bleeding" heart to his mistress, receives a gift from her:

You in requital gave a stone,
Not easie to be broken;
An Embleme sure that of your own
Hearts hardnesse was a token.

The lady of "Song: Go, Cruel Maid" is described as unattainable in the characteristic Petrarchan fashion. Typical also is her "heart of Ice," which threatens the death of the lover.

The designation of these lyrics as conventional and as typically Petrarchan does not imply that they are inferior poems. All contain lively images, and each is a small but delightful comment about one or another aspect of unrequited love. But none of them succeeds in making the reader completely believe in the speaker's plight; all seem to be written as exercises on the theme of the cruel-fair. In one of the poems written at least in part in the Petrarchan mode, however, Felltham strikes a note of sincerity. In "Song: Now (as I live) I love thee much," the speaker expresses the fear that if he causes the lady to love him, she may later be disappointed because of his shortcomings. After arguing against the possibility of their relationship, the speaker concludes by paradoxically protesting his love for the lady: "Were't not a love beyond excesse,/It might be more." The situation is closely akin to that of the stereotyped Petrarchan lover, but it is somewhat more complex. The speaker is concerned not that the lady will scorn him but that she will love him and be disappointed because he cannot provide her with all she deserves. He also is fearful lest he create a situation in which he himself may be hurt.

Felltham also gained freshness of expression in some Petrarchan lyrics by the addition of that peculiar cleverness which characterized seventeenth-century wit. Describing Cupid and Venus as "A Boy and a common Tit," the poet employs wit in the service of humor in "Song: Cupid and Venus" when he proves "That *Vulcan* onely is the god of Love." Felltham also complains wittily of the faithlessness of women in his song "Upon a breach of Promise" in which the poet is "confirm'd" in his belief that "No Woman hath a soul." Employing alchemical imagery, reminiscent of Donne's, the poem concludes that,

> So though they seem to cheer, and speak
> Those things we most implore.
> They do but flame us up to break,
> Then never mind us more.

Through the use of wit in "The Spring in the Rock," Felltham points a *carpe diem* lesson so popular with the Cavalier poets of the mid-seventeenth century: seize each day for life is short. The lover begins the poem by telling his lady a fable about a coy mistress who was turned into a rock, and the moral of the fable warns the "Harsh Maid" to ". . . take heed then, repent and know/They that chang'd her can alter you." The *carpe diem* theme is explicitly stated in "To Phryne," for the speaker tells Phryne that, when her youth and beauty are gone, "Then wilt thou sighing lye,/Repent and smart, and so by two deaths dye."

In these last few poems Felltham's attitude toward love has moved some distance from that of the ever worshipful, ever rejected Petrarchan. As did most poets of the seventeenth century, Felltham believed that a fulfilling relationship between men and women had to be reciprocal and, while love might be idealistic, that idealism had to have its foundation in actuality. The revolt against the artificial and unrealistic Italianate tradition was led by two men of widely differing personalities and talents, Ben Jonson and John Donne. Despite their differences, which were considerable, both poets saw that the lyric, to continue as a meaningful genre, had to convey rational, highly personal explorations of that unity underlying the bewildering diversity of human experience. Although both handled the many aspects of love thoroughly and frankly, their forms of expression differed. Jonson wrote clear and restrained verse of a high polish; Donne's is often complex and passionate, and his poetry avoids the easy smoothness of Elizabethan versification. Felltham was influenced, as were many other poets of the 1630s and 1640s, by both the Classical and Metaphysical models.[25] From his friend Ben Jonson he borrowed clarity of statement and a concern for beauty of expression. From the Dean of St. Paul's he took the metaphysical attitude and the passionate paradoxical metaphor. With these borrowed characteristics, he produced six highly polished metaphysical love lyrics.

A Neoplatonic view of love underlies all six: desire begins with the admiration of physical beauty, it progresses to a contemplation of spiritual worth, and it culminates in the union of the souls of the lover and his beloved.[26] Felltham traces these stages of love and explores the various trials that beset lovers as they seek to achieve a perfect mingling of their souls; and his poems "The Cause," "The Vow-breach," "The Sympathy," "The Reconcilement," and "A Farewell" together form a narrative reflecting these common Neoplatonic attitudes. The speaker of "The Cause" asserts that his and Clarissa's relationship involves a mingling of their souls. Clarissa, in the enigmatic "The Vow-breach," confesses a lapse which she implores her lover not to specify. It becomes clear in "The Sympathy" that the lady's breach is her doubt, her "heretick thoughts" about their love; but the lover proves by his example of the sympathetic lutes that he and his lady are "Two souls Co-animate." In "The Reconcilement," the speaker declares that Clarissa's "loose and wandring fears" have been purged and that she is thus created anew; and he invites her to join him in "close united Extasie." The series is concluded by "A Farewell," in which the lover declares that, when separated from her, he is "but as scatter'd dew/Till re-exhal'd again to Vertue; You." With the possible exception of "The Vow-breach," each of these poems can, of course, be read without reference to the other poems in the narrative; but all gain by their context.

"The Cause" begins by denying physical attraction as the sole object of desire: "Think not, Clarissa, I love thee/For thy meer outside, though it be/A Heaven more clear than that men cloudless see." The greater attraction is that of his lady's soul: "we may mix there/Like two Perfumes in the soft air,/And as chast Incense play above the sphere." The spiritual love shared by the two leads them upward "To clearer heights" until they "centre *Jove*." This double reference to Jupiter as both a planet and a god leads naturally to the metaphysical image which concludes the poem: "For when two souls shall towre so high,/Without their flesh their rayes shall flye,/Like Emanations from a Deity." "The Cause" is one of Felltham's finest poems, for this celebration of spiritual love is perfectly unified in imagery and beautifully simple in statement. The theme of the poem and its images are reminiscent of those found in Donne's "The Canonization," "The Anniversarie," and "The Relique"; but Felltham creates of them a wholly convincing personal statement.

In "The Vow-breach," one of the most elusive of Felltham's love poems, Clarissa has somehow broken trust; but she implores that her lapse not be revealed:

> if thou then
> Call back remembrance with her light agen
> Know thou art cruel: For those rayes to me
> (Like flashes wherewithall the Damned see
> Their plagues) become another Hell.

A strong tension results from the juxtaposition of unusual metaphors: darkness is good, light is evil; the former is the charity of silence, the latter the cruelty of gossip. And the almost Dantean lightning of remembrance is extended to provide the vehicle of the curse in the closing lines:

> For my whole Sex, when they shall find their shame
> Told in my Vow-breach by thy fatal name;
> Their spleen shal all in one eye pointed be,
> And then like Lightning darted all on thee.

Despite the elusiveness of the actual offense, which is not made clear until "The Sympathy," "The Vow-breach" is an effective poem; the feeling objectified in its images gives every impression of being strong and sincere.

"The Sympathy," which is much more complex in verse form than "The Cause" or "The Vow-breach," is carefully and sensitively designed to purge Clarissa's "heretick thoughts" by proving that the

lovers are "Two souls Co-animate." The central image of the poem
is clever in the metaphysical manner, yet wholly appropriate:

> Two Lutes are strung,
> And on a Table tun'd alike for song;
> Strike one, and that which none did touch,
> Shall sympathizing sound as much
> As that which toucht you see.
> Think then this world (which Heaven inroules)
> Is but a Table round, and souls
> More apprehensive be.

The poem concludes by reminding Clarissa that, even in physical
union, spiritual love can mix entwined hearts, thus allowing lovers to
boast that no absence can affect their love:

> Judge hence then our estate,
> Since when we lov'd there was not put
> Two earthen hearts in one brest, but
> Two souls Co-animate.

This celebration of spiritual love is again similar to passages by
Donne and other seventeenth-century poets. Yet Felltham's poem is
not merely derivative; it is certainly worthy of being admitted to the
canon of frequently anthologized Metaphysical poetry.

Coming immediately after "The Sympathy," "The Reconcilement" even more forcefully knits the lovers' souls together.
Clarissa's "loose and wandring fears" have been purged by
"penitential tears," and she is "new created." The lover concludes
with an invitation to join him in a sensuous mingling of their souls:

> Come then, and let us like two streams swell'd high,
> Meet, and with soft and gentle struglings try,
> How like their curling waves we mingle may,
> Till both be made one floud; then who can say
> Which this way flow'd, which that: For there will be
> Still water; close united Extasie.
> That when we next shall but of motion dream,
> We both shall slide one way, both make one stream.

"The Reconcilement," with its marvelous joining of religious and
erotic metaphors, beautifully records the reunion of lovers.

Calling to mind yet another famous poem of Donne's, Felltham's

"A Farewell" explores the problem inherent in the physical separa-
tions that lovers frequently must undergo:

> When by sad fate from hence I summon'd am,
> Call it not Absence, that's too mild a name.
> Believe it, dearest Soul, I cannot part,
>
> . . . .
>
> No; say I am dissolv'd: for as a Cloud
> By the Suns vigour melted is, and strow'd
> On the Earths face, to be exhal'd again
> To the same beams that turn'd it into rain.
> So absent think me but as scatter'd dew.
> Till re-exhal'd again to Vertue; You.

This poem, metaphysical in its surprising and unexpectedly apt
metaphor, is simply stated, tender in its sense of restrained drama.

Only one of Felltham's poems, the love lyric "When, Dearest, I
but think on thee," has enjoyed any wide audience; and, ironically,
it has done so in part because its authorship has so persistently been
attributed to Sir John Suckling. The lyric seems to have been circulated widely in manuscript, and a copy found among Suckling's
papers after his death was published in that Cavalier's *Last Remains*.[27] Felltham called attention to the mistaken attribution in a
headnote to the poem in the 1661 *Lusoria*, but few critics and
anthologists seem to have noticed it. Despite frequent notes on the
poem's authorship published during the nineteenth and early twentieth centuries,[28] some editors still assign the poem to Suckling[29];
and ironically, some critics have considered the poem to be one of
Suckling's finest.[30]

"When, Dearest, I but think on thee" does indeed deserve praise.
The dramatic situation is a common one, the physical separation of
lovers. Felltham, however, treats the old theme with freshness and
restrained vitality:

> When, Dearest, I but think on thee,
> Methinks all things that lovely be
>   Are present, and my soul delighted:
> For beauties that from worth arise,
> Are like the grace of Deities,
>   Still present with us, though unsighted.

Thus while I sit and sigh the day,
With all his spreading lights away,
    Till nights black wings do overtake me:
Thinking on thee, thy beauties then,
As sudden lights do sleeping men,
    So they by their bright rayes awake me.

Thus absence dyes, and dying proves
No absence can consist with Loves
    That do partake of fair perfection:
Since in the darkest night they may
By their quick motion find a way
    To see each other by reflection.

The waving Sea can with such floud,
Bath some high Palace that hath stood
    Far from the Main up in the River:
Oh think not then but love can do
As much, for that's an Ocean too,
    That flows not every day, but ever.

"When, Dearest, I but think on thee" represents the best blending possible of the techniques of Donne and Jonson. The divine quality of true love, the impossibility of any real absence, and the ingenious comparisons are elements the poet inherited from Donne; the urbane restraint, quiet confidence, melodic diction, and a regular, "singable" form are part of Jonson's legacy. "When, Dearest, I but think on thee" is one of the most beautiful minor poems of the period.

Considering the fact that Felltham wrote relatively few poems, his range is particularly noteworthy. His poems include a distinguished collection of love lyrics and a body of occasional poetry in which are represented almost all the subgenres popular in the earlier seventeenth century — from the epitaph and elegy to the "instructions to the painter" poem. Although not uniformly successful, most of these poems share a highly developed sense of dramatic tension, a tendency toward Baroque virtuosity, and a talent for the strikingly beautiful phrase. Felltham's sense of dramatic tension is best seen in his juxtaposition of contradictory attitudes held simultaneously, as in the poem on Buckingham; his personification of abstractions, as in the presentation of Death gently embracing Lady Venetia Digby; and his sense of restrained vitality in the more tender love lyrics. Felltham's tendency toward the Baroque is evident, for example, in the overstatement in the poem on Lord Coventry, the elegy on King Charles, and the lines on the Gentlewoman whose nose was pitted with smallpox. His penchant for the arrestingly beautiful phrase is exemplified throughout the poems.

Felltham, admittedly a minor writer, reveals in his poetry the richness of milieu which produced some of the greatest occasional and lyric poets in the English language. Felltham's measure as a poet is not his originality but his ability to make fresh and personal poems which derive from so fertile a milieu. His may not be a totally distinctive voice, but it is a fine one nevertheless. Poems such as "When, Dearest, I but think on thee," "The Cause," "The Sympathy," "On the Duke of Buckingham . . . ," "To the Memory of immortal Ben," and others merit for Felltham more recognition as a poet than he has heretofore received. He has no claim to status beyond that of minor poet, but such a ranking in a period as rich in poetry as the seventeenth century is hardly one to be despised.

CHAPTER 5

The Vicissitudes of Fashion

I The First Three Centuries

FELLTHAM'S reputation has fluctuated between modest interest and complete neglect in the more than three hundred and
fifty years since he first published prose and poetry. In his own century, Felltham was known and obviously respected by a large
number of readers. *Resolves: Divine, Morall, Politicall* went through
eleven editions before 1700. It was so well known by 1641 that
Abraham Cowley could refer in his play *The Guardian* to "he that
writ the Resolves" (act 4, sc. 7) and reasonably expect the members
of the audience — including, at the first performance, the future
King Charles II — to recognize the allusion. *A Brief Character of the
Low-Countries* was included in the last four seventeenth-century
editions of *Resolves* and was, in various versions, including a Dutch
translation, printed independently at least ten other times during the
period. It was widely imitated; by 1666, characters were written
about France, Italy, Spain, and even England and the colony of
Maryland. During the century of their composition, Felltham's
poems appeared in various printed collections, were included in four
editions of *Resolves*, and were circulated widely in manuscript.
Many seventeenth-century writers, most notable among them Henry
Vaughan, borrowed images, lines, and even long passages from
Felltham's prose and poetry for use in their own works.

Three important critical statements were made about Felltham's
works in his own century — in Thomas Randolph's poem on
Resolves (published 1638, but written earlier), in Gerard
Langbaine's *English Dramatic Poets* (1691), and in Anthony à
Wood's *Athenæ Oxonienses* (1691 - 1692). Randolph praises
Resolves for its worthy sentiments and its Senecan style and con-
cludes that the author himself must be a good man. Langbaine and

Wood not only mention Felltham as a poet, but place him among the chief poets writing during the 1630s.

In the eighteenth century, Felltham's reputation suffered a severe decline. *Resolves* — including the character of Holland and the poems — was published only once (1709); *A Brief Character* was issued as a separate work twice (the Dutch translation was reprinted in 1708 and the English original in 1770); and the lyric "When, Dearest, I but think on thee" was included in several editions of Sir John Suckling's works. Only one critic commented on Felltham and his work during the century: in *Reflections upon Accuracy of Style*, John Constable condemned the prose of *Resolves* as "too violent . . . forced and artificial"; and he called Felltham's more extended metaphors "tiresome lengths of childishness and affectation. . . ."[1] The eighteenth century was, however, an age in which critics considered some of Shakespeare's imagery too fantastic, and an Augustan naturally found Felltham's prose forbidding. Of Felltham's poetry, the eighteenth century had nothing at all to say, except to notice the "Answer" to Ben Jonson.

The nineteenth century was kinder to Felltham and his work but perhaps in the wrong way. Eight editions of *Resolves* — a few including some poems — were published between 1800 and 1840, two of them in the United States; selections from the book appeared in two important anthologies; an American magazine serialized *A Brief Character;* a few of the poems were printed in various places; several critical reviews of Felltham's works appeared in British and American periodicals; Felltham began to be noticed by literary historians; and some attempt was made to collect biographical information.[2] Unfortunately, the versions of Felltham's works that saw print during the period are cut, modernized, rearranged, and otherwise distorted; and the interest shown in them is almost always condescending.

This nineteenth-century resurgence of interest in Felltham is easily explained: the age interested itself both in the pious and in the antique, and Felltham's *Resolves* satisfied both interests. Nearly all of the critical estimates of Felltham's work during the period center on *Resolves*, about which two points are invariably made: "the work has an eminent tendency to advance the interests of sound Religion and Morality,"[3] and "The book before us is a Cabinet in the fashion of the day; full of gorgeous ornaments of mother of pearl and shells; and is curiously carved, braced, and hinged."[4] The book's moral value and its quaint style fascinated the nineteenth-century

reviewer, and the approximately half dozen lengthy periodical considerations of Felltham and *Resolves* focus exclusively on these two
themes.

Literary historians were not always so kind, however. None seems
to have known his poems; and, from remarks made about *Resolves*,
several of the writers had not even bothered to glance at Felltham's
essays. Although one notable literary historian did read Felltham, he
was perhaps the Victorian least temperamentally attuned to
seventeenth-century prose. Henry Hallam, the choleric father of
Alfred Tennyson's "A. H. H.," considered Felltham to be "not only
a labored and artificial, but a shallow writer. . . . one of our worst
writers in point of style."[5] George Saintsbury had a slightly higher
opinion of *Resolves*, but — like many another nineteenth- and
twentieth-century literary historian and critic — he insisted on the
misleading comparison of Felltham's book to Bacon's collection of
essays and asserted that *Resolves* was "far less magniloquent."[6]

II   *The Twentieth Century*

Twentieth-century readers have discovered in the literature of the
seventeenth century an immediacy and a relevance that strike a
responsive note. The works of such important seventeenth-century
artists as William Shakespeare, Sir Francis Bacon, John Donne, Ben
Jonson, Robert Herrick, George Herbert, Sir Thomas Browne, Andrew Marvell, and Henry Vaughan have been appreciated in the
twentieth century for their psychological subtlety, conscious artistry,
and profound vision of human possibilities. Owen Felltham, admittedly a minor writer, shares with his more important contemporaries these same qualities, though to a lesser degree. His relative
obscurity in the twentieth century results from the greater attention
paid to better-known writers, rather than from any inability on his
part to speak to modern concerns. This neglect is regrettable, not
only because of Felltham's intrinsic excellence, but also because
minor writers often reflect the temper of their times better than do
major figures. Fortunately, the tempo of Felltham scholarship and
criticism has quickened considerably in recent years.

The twentieth century began rather badly for Felltham with
Oliphant Smeaton's wholly unsatisfactory Temple Classics edition of
Resolves in 1904, a badly modernized and incomplete text with
superficial, inadequate, and often misleading annotations.[7] Fortunately, the book's critics were more responsible than its editor. In
his 1915 study *The English Essay and Essayists*, Hugh Walker

treated *Resolves* sympathetically and at some length, although he
overemphasized Bacon's influence on Felltham.[8] A decade later,
E. N. S. Thompson discussed the genre and style of *Resolves* in his
important monograph *The Seventeenth-Century English Essay*. He
noted that the 1628 excogitations do not follow "the precise style of
the resolve" and that some of the epigrammatic statements of the
1623 pieces "can hardly be carried in solution"; but he concluded
that many passages in Felltham's book "are written with real
beauty."[9]

   In 1928 Donald Cornu provided a useful scholarly and critical tool
in his doctoral dissertation, "A Biography and Bibliography of Owen
Felltham." Although he failed to discover many of the early editions
of *Low-Countries*, Cornu carefully described the seventeenth-
century editions of *Resolves*, and he corrected several errors and
filled in many lacunae in Felltham's biography. His research was
augmented in the 1930s and 1940s by Fred S. Tupper, who discovered the date and circumstances of Felltham's death and burial,[10]
and by Jean Robertson, who published materials of both
biographical and bibliographical significance.[11]

   In Douglas Bush, who is one of America's most distinguished
students of seventeenth-century English literature, Felltham found a
critic both discerning and sympathetic. In his authoritative *English
Literature in the Earlier Seventeenth Century*, first published in
1945, Bush devotes surprisingly generous space to a discussion of
Resolves and its author. Prizing Felltham's personality and style —
"the familiar essayist's capital" — he emphasizes the moderation,
virtue, charity, Christian Stoicism, and good sense of *Resolves*. Bush
uncondescendingly links Felltham with Sir Thomas Browne and
reminds the reader that it was Felltham who first saw the soul as "a
shoot of everlastingnesse," a phrase borrowed in Henry Vaughan's
poem "The Retreate."[12] Bush's perceptive appreciation may be the
most important single herald of the recent revival of interest in
Felltham. Another influential study is the 1953 article by McCrea
Hazlett which points out the changes made in style and genre in the
progressive stages of *Resolves* and argues that the additions and
revisions reflect Felltham's growing concern with persuading his
readers. Hazlett's study contains sensitive analyses of individual essays and suggests for Felltham an influential place in the development of the essay.[13]

   Recently, Felltham has been the center of a modest flurry of
critical and scholarly activity. Editors have begun with greater fre-

quency to include Felltham's poetry and prose in anthologies;[14] and his work has been the subject of doctoral dissertations.[15] His poems have been collected in a well-received and widely distributed edition.[16] An annotated bibliography considerably more extensive than Donald Cornu's has been published.[17] And the Canadian scholar Richard F. Kennedy is preparing a critical edition of *Resolves* for Oxford University's Clarendon Press. In *The Elected Circle*, an important study of prose art which considers only eight writers from John Donne to T. S. Eliot, Laurence Stapleton devotes a chapter entitled "The Graces and the Muses" to Owen Felltham.[18] Virtue was Felltham's muse; but, Stapleton points out, he also assiduously courted the graces, those jealous custodians of artistic expression. Her analysis of Felltham's stylistic accomplishments and her telling contrast of Bacon's essays with Felltham's are excellent. And Stapleton's sensitive critical appreciation of *Resolves'* graceful and charitable vision points up Felltham's enduring worth as a writer.

Despite the recent renewed interest in Felltham, much remains to be done. *A Brief Character of the Low-Countries* needs a new edition; when it is widely read, it will take a place of modest distinction among the comic and satiric works of its era. When his poems, which embrace most of the public and private genres popular in the earlier seventeenth century, are thoroughly studied and appreciated, Felltham will undoubtedly be accorded a reputation at least as great as that of Lord Herbert of Cherbury, Henry King, Thomas Carew, and other minor writers whose works have so far received much more attention than his. *Resolves: Divine, Morall, Politicall* is a rich mine for those interested in genre, in prose style, in Christian Stoicism, in Anglican theology, and in English translations of Latin poetry. *Resolves* is a delightful book, a lively compendium that deserves a place beside the works of Sir Thomas Browne and Robert Burton's *The Anatomy of Melancholy*. Most of all, Felltham's works need to be read. They have much to recommend them — humanity, wit, and style — more than enough to repay the effort of the specialist and the general reader alike.

Notes and References

Chapter One

1. The account in this chapter is based on M. Donald Cornu, "A Biography and Bibliography of Owen Felltham" (Ph. D. diss., University of Washington, 1928), supplemented and corrected by Jean Robertson, "Owen Felltham of Great Billing," *Notes and Queries* 173 (1937), 381 - 84; Fred S. Tupper, "New Facts Regarding Owen Feltham," *Modern Language Notes* 54 (1939), 199 - 201; and the author's research.

2. British Museum MS Harleian 1169 f. 81^r gives the residence of Thomas Felltham, Owen's father, as Mutford; and the Fellthams must have been living there in 1610 when Owen's brother Thomas was baptized (British Museum Add. MS 19129 f. 111^r).

3. The records are confused as to the order of the three sons. Harleian MS 1169 f. 81^r gives Thomas, "sonne & heire," as the first born, and he is followed by "Owyne" and "Robart." Davy's Suffolk Pedigrees (British Museum Add. MS 19129 f. 111^r) lists Thomas as son and heir, but gives his baptismal date as "13 Augt. 1610." in which case he either was younger than Owen or was not baptized until long after infancy. This same pedigree lists Robert as the second son and Owen as the third. The will of their father Thomas (P. C. C. Registered *Audley* 64) names Robert as the sole executor and heir to everything after all debts are paid, seeming to indicate that he was the firstborn. The author is grateful to Edmund Miller of The Bronx, New York, for pointing out that the seventeenth-century engraved title pages of *Resolves* which reproduce the Felltham coat of arms add to it a crescent, the usual cadency mark of a second son.

4. MS Harleian 1169 f. 81^r.

5. British Museum MS Harleian 5861 f. 76^v.

6. Sir William Corwallis, *Essays*, ed. D. C. Allen (Baltimore, 1946), p. xiii.

7. This is the only record in print of Felltham's having spelled his given name with an "i." Although his surname appears a few times during the seventeenth century with only one "l", he most commonly spelled it with two. For that reason "Felltham" is used throughout this work. Several

nineteenth- and twentieth-century reviewers, anthologists, critics, and editors spell the name "Feltham"; and that spelling is preserved in direct quotations from their works. During the seventeenth century, the name was probably pronounced "Feltone" (see E. V., "Felltham Family," *Notes and Queries*, 4th Series, 9 [1872], 307).

8. Anonymous review, *Meliora* 4 (1862), 92.

9. Ibid.

10. G. E. Cokayne, *The Complete Peerage*, rev. and enlarged by Geoffrey H. White, 12 vols. (London, 1910 - 1959), vol.12, pt. 1, 708 - 9. Previous biographers of Felltham supposed that the O'Briens, Royalist and Anglican, were probably attracted to the young Felltham because of the strong statements in *Resolves* supporting King and Established Church. If such were the case, the O'Briens obviously vacillated during the Civil War since Barnabas O'Brien claimed to have spent 16,000 pounds in the Parliamentary cause, and Henry Cromwell rewarded the family for services rendered (see Albert Frederick Pollard, "Barnabas O'Brien, *"Dictionary of National Biography)*. Felltham, however, remained Royalist and Anglican.

11. Mary, Dowager Countess of Thomond (baptized 12 March 1591/2, died 1675) was married first to Lord Chrichton of Sanquhar (hanged in 1612 for killing his fencing master) and later to Barnabas O'Brien, sixth Earl of Thomond (born about 1590). By her second husband she had two children, Henry (1621-1691) and Penelope, Countess of Peterborough (died 1702).

12. Unfortunately, the earliest extant birth, marriage, and death records of St. Andrew's Church, Great Billing, begin with the year 1662. In 1967, the Rev. W. B. Spenser, rector of St. Andrew's, kindly searched those records to the end of the seventeenth century and found no mention of anyone named Felltham.

13. Cornu, "A Biography and Bibliography of Owen Felltham," pp. 101 - 102.

14. P. C. C. Registered *Hene* 46, proved 22 April 1668.

15. Quoted from *The Poems of Owen Felltham*, ed. Ted-Larry Pebworth and Claude J. Summers (University Park, Pennsylvania, 1973), p. 68; the translation is editorial.

Chapter Two

1. All quotations from the Short Century of *Resolves* follow the text of the first edition (1623), with the titles of the individual pieces supplied from the third edition (1628B); quotations from the Long Century follow the text of the second edition (1628A); and quotations from the Revised Short Century follow the text of the eighth edition (1661). The two allegorical designs used for the engraved title pages of the seventeenth-century editions of *Resolves* are illustrated in Ted-Larry Pebworth, "An Annotated Bibliography of Owen Felltham," *Bulletin of the New York Public Library* 79 (1976), 212 - 13.

2. McCrea Hazlett, " 'New Frame and Various Composition'; Development in the Form of Owen Felltham's *Resolves*," *Modern Philology* 51 (1953), 96.

3. Douglas Bush, *English Literature in the Earlier Seventeenth Century, 1600 - 1660*, 2nd ed. rev. (Oxford, 1962). p. 202.

4. For a valuable discussion of the impact of science on the age, see C. M. Coffin, *John Donne and the New Philosophy* (New York, 1937).

5. Bush, *English Literature in the Earlier Seventeenth Century*, p. 202.

6. Ibid., p. 201.

7. McCrea Hazlett's study, cited above, contains valuable analyses of individual resolves in a chronological framework; but where Hazlett regards the changes in form that were effected as *Resolves* underwent expansion and revision as reflections of Felltham's growing concern with persuading his readers, the ensuing discussion argues that the changes in form represent shifts in genre from the resolve (1623), through the meditation (1628), to the personal essay (1661).

8. Joseph Hall, *Works*, rev. ed., 12 vols. (Oxford, 1837), VIII, 5.

9. Elbert N. S. Thompson, *The Seventeenth-Century English Essay*, University of Iowa Humanistic Studies, vol. 3 (1926), 72. M. W. Black, in his *Richard Braithwait* (Philadelphia, 1928), does not attribute *Sundry Christian Resolves* to that author.

10. For example, Richard Garnett and Edmund Gosse, *English Literature: An Illustrated Record* (New York, 1905), III, 5. For the development of the character in England, see Benjamin Boyce, *The Theophrastan Character in England to 1642* (Cambridge, Massachusetts, 1947).

11. George Williamson, *The Senecan Amble* (Chicago, 1951), p. 203.

12. First published in the posthumously issued works of Thomas Randolph, *Poems with the Mvses Looking-Glasse: And amyntas* (1638). Quoted from the text in G. Thorn-Drury, ed., *The Poems of Thomas Randolph* (London, 1929), pp. 75 - 78.

13. Williamson, *The Senecan Amble*, p. 202.

14. For example, the anonymous reviews in *Gentleman's Magazine* 91, New Series 14 (1821), 56; *Retrospective Review* 10 (1824), 345; and *American Monthly Review* 1 (1832), 454.

15. But see Hazlett, "New Frame and Various Composition," p. 101.

16. Sir Herbert J. C. Grierson, ed., *Metaphysical Lyrics & Poems of the Seventeenth Century* (Oxford, 1921), p. xxxvii.

17. Hazlett, "New Frame and Various Composition," p. 96.

18. Ibid.

19. Ibid.

20. Bush, *English Literature in the Earlier Seventeenth Century*, p. 198.

21. What is said about the meditation here does, of course, apply to those few Short Century resolves which have meditative sections of any length.

22. Hall, *Works*, VI, 61. The "forms of discourse" listed are chapter titles occurring on pp. 62 - 70. For an informative discussion of Hall's *The Arte of*

Divine Meditation, see Louis L. Martz, *The Poetry of Meditation: A Study in English Religious Literature of the Seventeenth Century* (New Haven, 1954).

23. For example, Roberta Brinkley, ed., *English Prose of the XVII Century* (New York, 1951); Alexander Witherspoon and Frank Warnke, eds., *Seventeenth-Century Prose and Poetry,* 2nd ed. (New York, 1963); and David Novarr, ed., *Seventeenth-Century English Prose* (New York, 1967).

24. For example, the anonymous reviews in *The London Christian Instructor, or Congregational Magazine* 6 (1823), 377, and *American Monthly Review* (Boston), 1 (1832), 458; Henry Hallam, *Introduction to the Literature of Europe in the Fifteenth, Sixteenth, and Seventeenth Centuries* (Originally published 1837 - 1839), 4 vols. in 2 (New York, 1880), II, 150 - 51.

25. For each of the examples quoted (italics supplied), the *Oxford English Dictionary* cites Felltham's *Resolves* or plagiarisms from it (most notably the Earl of Manchester's *Al Mondo or Contemplations of Death and Immortality* [1631 and in later editions]) as the first recorded use. Although Jean Robertson, in "The Use Made of Owen Felltham's 'Resolves': A Study in Plagiarism," *Modern Language Review* 39 (1944), 115, asserts that Dr. Johnson cites several quotations from *Resolves* "with approval" in his famous *Dictionary,* examination of early editions of the *Dictionary* shows that Felltham is virtually ignored. It is not surprising, since Dr. Johnson disliked neologisms. The inclusion of Felltham in the *Dictionary* dates from 1818 when the Rev. Henry Todd revised and enlarged Johnson's work. For an extended, though not complete, list of Felltham's neologisms, see Richard F. Kennedy, "Words from Owen Felltham," *Notes and Queries* 216 (1971), 4 - 12.

26. These are the sixty-two pairs of corresponding essays. The left-hand number in each pair is the 1623 resolve; the right-hand one, the 1661 essay made from it: 1, 1; 2, 2; 3, 3; 4, 4; 5, 5; 7, 6; 9, 7; 10, 8; 11, 9; 12, 10; 13, 11; 14, 12; 15, 14; 16, 13; 17, 15; 20, 20; 21, 50; 22, 47; 23, 21; 25, 22; 26, 23; 27, 27; 28, 24; 29, 25; 30, 26; 31, 28; 33, 29; 34, 30; 35, 31; 36, 32; 37, 33; 38, 34; 39, 35; 40, 37; 42, 39; 43, 40; 46, 41; 47, 43; 48, 44; 49, 42; 50, 45; 51, 49; 52, 46; 54, 48; 56, 51; 58, 52; 59, 53; 61, 55; 62, 57; 63, 56; 67, 59; 72, 60; 75, 63; 77, 77; 82, 69; 84, 64; 86, 72; 88, 78; 89, 66; 92, 74; 93, 68; 98, 81.

Those 1623 resolves discarded in the 1661 revision are numbers 6, 8, 18, 19, 24, 32, 41, 44, 45, 53, 55, 57, 60, 64, 65, 66, 68, 69, 70, 71, 73, 74, 76, 78, 79, 80, 81, 83, 85, 87, 90, 91, 94, 95, 96, 97, 99, 100. Those essays wholly new in 1661 are numbers 16, 17, 18, 19, 36, 38, 54, 58, 61, 62, 65, 67, 70, 71, 73, 75, 76, 79, 80, 82, 83, 84, 85. These lists differ somewhat from those of Hazlett ("New Frame and Various Composition," p. 93n); he lists only fifty-eight pairs, failing to see the other four.

27. Bush, *English Literature in the Earlier Seventeenth Century,* p. 194.

28. Morris W. Croll, "The Baroque Style in Prose," in *"Attick" & Baroque Prose Style,* ed. J. Max Patrick and Robert O. Evans with John M. Wallace (Princeton, 1969), p. 210.

29. Most of these are discussed in Thompson, *The Seventeenth-Century English Essay.*

30. See Ted-Larry Pebworth, "Jonson's *Timber* and the Essay Tradition," in *Essays in Honor of Esmond Linworth Marilla,* ed. Thomas A. Kirby and W. John Olive (Baton Rouge, 1970), pp. 115 - 26.

31. Albert Feuillerat, ed., *The Prose Works of Sir Philip Sidney,* 4 vols., (Cambridge, 1912; reprinted 1963), III, 25.

32. Paragraphing appears for the first time in *Resolves* in the twenty-three new pieces of the Revised Short Century. The brief resolves of 1623 and the longer excogitations of 1628 are not paragraphed, although some of the latter might profitably have been broken into smaller units. In the new essays in the Revised Short Century, all of which are quite lengthy, Feltham makes good use of paragraphing to indicate divisions within his overall subjects and to emphasize the progressive steps toward his conclusions.

33. Laurence Stapleton, "The Graces and the Muses: Feltham's *Resolves,*" in *The Elected Circle: Studies in the Art of Prose* (Princeton, 1973), p. 91.

Chapter Three

1. For a discussion of the character as a genre and for the modifications of it in English, see Chapter 2, Section II above. In addition to Benjamin Boyce's *The Theophrastan Character in England to 1642,* cited in Chapter 2, that same author's *The Polemic Character: 1640 - 1661* (Lincoln, Nebraska, 1955) is of particular relevance here.

2. A corrupt text was printed, without attribution, in 1647 as *Terrible Nevves from Scotland;* a better text, bearing the more common title appeared in 1649 (erroneously attributed to James Howell on the title page) and in 1659 (without attribution). Printed and bound up with pirated editions of Feltham's *Low-Countries* (which appears under the title *Batavia: Or The Hollander displayed*), *Scotland* was reissued frequently after the Restoration. Sir Walter Scott, in his *Secret History of the Court of James the First* (London, 1811), II, 73 - 89, was the first editor to attribute *Scotland* to Weldon. For a denial of Howell's authorship of the work, see William Harvey Vann, *Notes on the Writings of James Howell* (Waco, Texas, 1924), pp. 66 - 67.

3. For Henry Seile's testimony concerning the date of composition, presumably recording Feltham's own statement on the subject, see Section II of this chapter below. No evidence of a Dutch journey appears in the Short Century of *Resolves* (1623), whereas the excogitations of the Long Century (1628) contain several allusions indicating firsthand knowledge of Holland and its inhabitants. The freshness of detail in *Low-Countries* supports the conclusion that it was written during or shortly after the trip itself.

4. Copies in British Museum MS Harleian 5111 and Huntington Library MS 14201 are prefaced by identical letters dated "Egipt this 22: Jannar:" and signed "J. S."; see Jean Robertson, "Feltham's *Character of the Low*

Countries," *Modern Language Notes* 58 (1943), 385 - 88, for the text of the letter.

5. The 1648 edition and the first state of the 1652 edition are erroneously designated *Three Moneths Obseruations of the Low-Countries;* the second state of the 1652 edition gives the title as *A true and exact Character of the Low-Countreyes.*

6. See Ted-Larry Pebworth, "The 'Character' in George Alsop's *Mary-Land,"* *Seventeenth-Century News* 34 (1976), in press.

7. All quotations from *Low-Countries* follow the text of the first authoritative edition (London: for Henry Seile, 1652).

8. Boyce, *The Polemic Character*, p. 45.

Chapter Four

1. Anthony à Wood, *Athenæ Oxonienses*, ed. Philip Bliss, 4 vols. (London, 1813 - 1820), IV, 222. This assessment, made between 1680 and 1690, lists the other important poets of the 1630s as Drayton, Randolph, Jonson, and Heywood.

2. Pebworth and Summers, eds., *The Poems of Owen Felltham*. All quotations from Felltham's poetry are from this edition; the translations are editorial.

3. See the group of poems entitled *Eupheme* in his *Underwoods*.

4. R. T. Petersson, *Sir Kenelm Digby: The Ornament of England, 1603 - 1665* (Cambridge, Massachusetts, 1956), p. 103.

5. Ibid.

6. Bush, *English Literature in the Earlier Seventeenth Century*, p. 124.

7. Alexander Witherspoon and Frank Warnke, eds., *Seventeenth-Century Prose and Poetry*, 2nd ed. (New York, 1963), p. 868.

8. Reproduced in C. H. Herford, Percy Simpson, and Evelyn Simpson, eds., *Ben Jonson*, 11 vols. (Oxford, 1925 - 1952), VI, 395.

9. Ibid., pp. 492 - 94; and Pebworth and Summers, eds., *The Poems of Owen Felltham*, Appendix A, pp. 80 - 81.

10. Gerard Langbaine, *English Dramatic Poets*, (Oxford, 1691), p. 301.

11. Herford and Simpson, eds., *Ben Jonson*, X, 331n.

12. Langbaine, *English Dramatic Poets*, p. 303n.

13. John Palmer, *Ben Jonson* (New York, 1934), pp. 275, 276.

14. Larry S. Champion, *Ben Jonson's 'Dotages': A Reconsideration of the Late Plays* (Lexington, Ky., 1967), p. 77.

15. Herford and Simpson, eds., *Ben Jonson*, I, 95.

16. Arthur Penrhyn Stanley, *Historical Memorials of Westminster Abbey*, 4th ed. rev. (London, 1876), p. 271.

17. Edmund Malone, ed., *The Plays and Poems of William Shakespeare*, 10 vols. in 11 (London, 1790), vol. I, pt. 1, p. 112n.

18. William Gifford, ed., *The Works of Ben Jonson*, 9 vols. (London, 1875; originally published 1816), I, cc.

19. Reproduced in Pebworth and Summers, eds., *The Poems of Owen Felltham*, Appendix B, pp. 82 - 83.

20. Jean Robertson, "The Poems of Owen Felltham," *Modern Language Notes* 58 (1943), 389.

21. For a detailed study of this subject, see Lu Emily Pearson, *Elizabethan Love Conventions* (Berkeley, California, 1933).

22. See, for example, the entries in Pepys' *Diary*, 23 September 1667 and 27 January 1667/8.

23. What little is known of the poem's authorship and the facts of its manuscript and printing history are detailed in the textual note to Felltham's "Answer" in Pebworth and Summers, eds., *The Poems of Owen Felltham*, p. 46.

24. Cornu, "A Biography and Bibliography of Owen Felltham," p. 83.

25. One of the best analyses of Jonson's technique is Ralph S. Walker's "Ben Jonson's Lyric Poetry," *Criterion* 13 (1933 - 1934), 430 - 48. The classic study of Donne's technique is Pierre Legouis' *Donne the Craftsman* (Paris, 1928). For an illuminating discussion of the complementary influences of Jonson and Donne on the poetry of the earlier seventeenth century, see the first chapter of J. B. Leishman's *The Monarch of Wit* (London, 1951; reprinted New York, 1966).

26. For the sources of this concept, see A. J. Smith, "The Metaphysics of Love," *Review of English Studies*, New Series, 9 (1958), 362 - 75.

27. *The Last Remains of S^r. John Suckling* (London, 1659), pp. 32 - 33.

28. For example, in Cumming's second edition of *Resolves* (London, 1820), pp. 452 - 53; G. Thorn-Drury, "Sir John Suckling," *Notes and Queries*, Eleventh Series, 1 (1910), 281; and Robert Pierpoint, " 'When, Dearest, I But Think of Thee': Song by Suckling or by Felltham," *Notes and Queries*, Eleventh Series, 6 (1912), 346.

29. For example, A. Hamilton Thompson, ed., *The Works of Sir John Suckling* (London, 1910; reprinted New York, 1964), pp. 67 - 68 of both printings; A. J. M. Smith, ed., *Seven Centuries of Verse*, 2nd ed. rev. and enlarged (New York, 1957), pp. 196 - 97.

30. For example, S. Austin Allibone, *A Critical Dictionary of English Literature*, 3 vols. (Philadelphia, 1891), II, 2298.

Chapter Five

1. John Constable, *Reflections upon Accuracy of Style* (London, 1734), pp. 72 - 73, 106.

2. For details of all but the anthologies, see Pebworth, "An Annotated Bibliography of Owen Felltham." The anthologies are George Burnett, ed., *Specimens of English Prose-Writers from the Earliest Times to the Close of the Seventeenth Century*, 3 vols. (London, 1807); and Henry Craik, ed., *English Prose Selections*, 5 vols. (New York, 1893 - 1896).

3. Anonymous review, *Gentleman's Magazine* 88 (1818), 347.

4. Anonymous review, *Gentleman's Magazine*, 91 (1821), 56.

5. Henry Hallam, *Introduction to the Literature of Europe in the Fifteenth, Sixteenth, and Seventeenth Centuries*, 4 vols. in 2 (New York, 1880; originally published in England 1837 - 1839), II, 150 - 51.

6. George Saintsbury, *A Short History of English Literature* (New York, 1898), p. 455.

7. [Oliphant Smeaton, ed.], *Resolves: Divine, Morall and Politicall* (London, 1904).

8. Hugh Walker, *The English Essay and Essayists* (London, 1915), pp. 63 - 66.

9. Thompson, *The Seventeenth-Century English Essay*, pp. 74 - 76.

10. Tupper, "New Facts Regarding Owen Feltham."

11. Robertson, "Owen Felltham of Great Billing"; "Felltham's *Character of the Low Countries*"; "The Poems of Owen Felltham"; and "The Use Made of Owen Felltham's 'Resolves': A Study in Plagiarism."

12. Bush, *English Literature in the Earlier Seventeenth Century* (Oxford, 1945), pp. 190 - 92; 2nd ed. rev. (Oxford, 1962), pp. 201 - 3.

13. Hazlett, "New Frame and Various Composition."

14. In addition to the anthologies cited in Chapter 2, n. 23 above, see Helen Gardner, ed., *the Metaphysical Poets* (Harmondsworth and Baltimore, 1957); and Frank Kermode and John Hollander, general eds., *The Oxford Anthology of English Literature* (New York and London, 1973).

15. For example, Hortense E. Thornton, "Owen Feltham: A Study in Seventeenth-Century Prose" (unpublished doctoral dissertation, Howard, 1970); and Barbara E. Bergquist, critical dissertation in progress, Pennsylvania.

16. Pebworth and Summers, eds., *The Poems of Owen Felltham*.

17. Pebworth, "An Annotated Bibliography of Owen Felltham."

18. Stapleton, *The Elected Circle*, pp. 73 - 92.

Selected Bibliography

PRIMARY SOURCES

1. Important Early Editions

Resolues: Diuine, Morall, Politicall. London: Henry Seile, [1623]. *STC* 10755. First edition; contains one hundred short, untitled pieces; referred to in this present work as the Short Century. Cited as 1623.

Resolves: A duple Century, one new an other of a second Edition. London: Henry Seile, 1628. *STC* 10756 and 10757. Contains, in addition to the Short Century, one hundred new and longer essays referred to in this present work as the Long Century. Cited as 1628A.

Resolves: A Duple Century, ye 3rd Edition. London: Henry Seile, 1628. *STC* 10758. Reverses the order of the Short and Long Centuries; adds titles to the pieces of the Short Century. Reprinted in this form 1631, 1634, 1636, and 1647. Cited as 1628B.

Resolves: The eight [sic] *Impression, With New, & Severall other Additions both in Prose, and Verse.* London: A[nne] Seile, 1661. Wing *STC* F655A. Contains, in addition to the unchanged Long Century, eighty-five essays which are revisions of and substitutions for the Short Century; referred to in this present work as the Revised Short Century. Bound into the volume are two discourses on Biblical passages and *Lusoria, Or Occasional Pieces,* the latter paged separately and consisting of forty-two poems, *A Brief Character of the Low-Countries,* and eighteen letters. Reprinted in this form 1670, 1677, and 1696. Cited as 1661.

Resolves: Divine, Moral, Political . . . this Twelfth Edition. London: Benjamin Motte, 1709. "Modernized" edition of the 1661 publication; includes "A Form of Prayer Compos'd for the Family of the Right Honorable the Countess of THOMOND."

2. Critical Editions

"A Critical Variorum Edition of Owen Felltham's *Resolves.*" Edited by Ted-Larry Pebworth, Ph.D. dissertation, Louisiana State University, 1966. This first inclusive edition takes into consideration all additions to and

changes made in the eight editions published during Felltham's
lifetime; the introduction includes a survey of criticism.
The Poems of Owen Felltham. Edited by Ted-Larry Pebworth and Claude J.
   Summers. Seventeenth-Century Editions and Studies No. 1. University Park, Pennsylvania: Seventeenth-Century News, 1973. The first
   separate edition of the poems and the only inclusive one. Biographical
   and critical introduction; textual and critical notes.

SECONDARY SOURCES

1. Biography and Bibliography

CORNU, MAX DONALD. "A Biography and Bibliography of Owen Felltham."
   Ph.D. dissertation, University of Washington, 1928. Most comprehen-
   sive work about the subject to that time; contains a few errors and
   omissions.
PEBWORTH, TED-LARRY. "An Annotated Bibliography of Owen Felltham."
   Bulletin of the New York Public Library 79 (1976), 209 - 24. Lists all
   editions and all significant scholarly and critical materials from 1623
   through 1973.
ROBERTSON, JEAN. "Owen Felltham of Great Billing." *Notes and Queries* 173
   (1937), 381 - 84. Concerns primarily the litigation between the
   Dowager Countess of Thomond and Felltham's heirs.
TUPPER, FRED S. "New Facts Regarding Owen Feltham." *Modern
   Language Notes* 54 (1939), 199 - 201. Concerns Felltham's service to
   Barnabas O'Brien and the circumstances surrounding Felltham's
   death and burial.

2. Critical and Scholarly Essays

Anonymous. "Owen Felltham and his 'Resolves.' " *Meliora* 4 (1862), 89 -
   103. Primarily biographical, but has some discussion of *Resolves* and
   the poems, praising the former for its insight, richness, and elegance
   of expression.
Anonymous. [Review.] *American Monthly Review* (Boston), 1 (1832), 451 -
   59. Discusses the point of view of *Resolves;* praises the use of
   metaphor and illustration, and the warmth, charm, and good sense of
   the book; damns the Senecan style and the neologisms. Praises the wit
   and humor of *Low-Countries*.
———. [Review.] *Gentleman's Magazine* 91, New Series 14 (1821), 55 - 56.
   Discusses *Resolves* as a work of casuistry; has an appreciative comment on the book's style.
———. [Review.] *The London Christian Instructor, or Congregational
   Magazine* 6 (1823), 375 - 79. Praises Felltham's imagination and the
   richness of language in *Resolves;* complains about frequency of an-
   tithesis and the fondness for neologisms.

————. [Review.] *Retrospective Review* 10 (1824), 343 - 55. Discusses briefly the resolve as a genre; praises the poetic use of metaphor and illustration in *Resolves;* points out Felltham's common sense, knowledge of mankind, and tolerance; recommends the book for the purity of its religious and moral principles.

DANIELS, R. BALFOUR. "Resolves of a Royalist." In *Some Seventeenth-Century Worthies in a Twentieth-Century Mirror.* Chapel Hill: University of North Carolina Press, 1940, pp. 140 - 44. Slight but appreciative survey of Felltham and his work.

HAZLETT, McCREA. " 'New Frame and Various Composition': Development in the Form of Owen Felltham's *Resolves.*" *Modern Philology* 51 (1953), 93 - 101. Discusses the changes made in style and genre from the original resolves of 1623 to the revisions of 1661.

PATRIDES, C. A. "Bacon and Feltham: Victims of Literary Piracy." *Notes and Queries,* New Series 5 (1958), 63 - 65. Points out plagiarism from *Resolves* by Robert Herne in his *Ros Coeli* (1640).

ROBERTSON, JEAN. "Felltham's *Character of the Low Countries.*" *Modern Language Notes* 58 (1943), 385 - 88. Discusses various manuscript copies of the work; comments on the vogue for characterizing nations in the middle of the seventeenth century.

————. "The Use Made of Owen Felltham's 'Resolves': A Study in Plagiarism." *Modern Language Review* 39 (1944), 108 - 15. Detailed readings from several seventeenth- and early eighteenth-century plagiarizers of *Resolves.*

STAPLETON, LAURENCE. "The Graces and the Muses: Felltham's *Resolves.*" In *The Elected Circle: Studies in the Art of Prose.* Princeton: Princeton University Press, 1973, pp. 73 - 92. Sensitive exploration of the interaction between style and meaning, including the limitations imposed by genre; stresses the Christianity rather than the Stoicism of *Resolves.*

3. Intellectual, Literary, and Political History of the Period

ASHLEY, MAURICE. *England in the Seventeenth Century (1603 - 1714).* The Pelican History of England, vol. 6. 2nd ed. Baltimore: Penguin Books Inc., 1954. One of the best one-volume political, religious, and social histories of the period.

BOYCE, BENJAMIN. *The Polemic Character: 1640 - 1661.* Lincoln: University of Nebraska Press, 1955; reprinted New York: Octagon Books, 1969. Survey of propagandistic characters written during the middle of the seventeenth century.

————. *The Theophrastan Character in England to 1642.* Cambridge: Harvard University Press, 1947; reprinted New York: Humanities Press, 1967. Discusses the origins of the genre and modifications of it made by English writers.

BUSH, DOUGLAS. *English Literature in the Earlier Seventeenth Century, 1600 - 1660.* 2nd ed. rev. Oxford: The Clarendon Press, 1962. Standard literary history of the period.

CROLL, MORRIS W. *"Attic" & Baroque Prose Style: The Anti-Ciceronian Movement.* Edited by J. Max Patrick and Robert O. Evans with John M. Wallace. Princeton: Princeton University Press, 1969. Important collection of essays on sixteenth- and seventeenth-century prose styles.

THOMPSON, E. N. S. *The Seventeenth-Century English Essay.* University of Iowa Humanistic Studies III. Iowa City: The University of Iowa, 1926; reprinted New York: Haskell House, 1967. Although faulty in some attributions and dates of publication, still the best study on the development of the genre.

TILLYARD, E. M. W. *The Elizabethan World Picture.* New York: Macmillan Company, 1943; reprinted New York: Vintage Books, 1961. Classic study of the Renaissance man's view of the cosmos and his inner self.

WILLIAMSON, GEORGE. *The Senecan Amble.* Chicago: The University of Chicago Press, 1951. Most detailed examination of this prose style ever made.

Index